Psychoanalytic and Psychotherapeutic Perspectives on Stepfamilies and Stepparenting

Psychoanalytic and Psychotherapeutic Perspectives on Stepfamilies and Stepparenting looks at the role stepparents can play in the psychic development of children. Stepparenting requires enormous confidence and resilience that stretches into a territory of human emotions and conflict that can make marriage seem easy. Prophecy Coles' concern has been that we are witnessing a new kinship system and our psychological thinking has not kept up with the emotional effect that stepparents are having upon the next generation.

The author traces the history of our beliefs about stepparents through the oral tradition of the fairy story into our present, arguably prejudiced beliefs about them. Coles explores whether our feelings about stepparents arise from the unconscious tradition that placed stepparents in hostile opposition to the natural forces of parenting. The absence of detailed clinical work on the subject has meant that the author has drawn on interviews, biography and three long-term research projects to think about this new family constellation.

Covering such topics as the prevalence and importance of stepmothers historically, the reasons for psychoanalytic neglect of this subject, and using clinical material drawn from work with stepmothers, children and fathers, this is a much-needed guide to working with families affected by maternal loss and alternative parenting roles. It will encourage a further appreciation of the psychological difficulties that stepparents face, and at the same time offer a re-appraisal of the pain that young children go through when their parents decide to separate. *Psychoanalytic and Psychotherapeutic Perspectives on Stepfamilies and Stepparenting* will appeal greatly to psychoanalysts and psychoanalytic psychotherapists.

Prophecy Coles is a retired psychotherapist. In all she has written she has been pursuing the question as to whether our childhood relationships, beyond those with our parents, such as those with siblings, nannies, wet nurses, grandparents, ancestors and now our stepparents, can leave a lasting impression that affects the way we relate to others in the world. Her publications include *The Importance of Sibling Relationships in Psychoanalysis* (2003), *Sibling Relationships* (2006), *The Uninvited Guest from the Unremembered Past* (2011) and *The Shadow of the Second Mother* (2015).

"Why hasn't the psychoanalytic world addressed the role and difficulties of stepparents in our society when almost half of our children now come from divorced families? Prophecy Coles lays bare the failure of her profession as she explores the reasons for the negative image given to stepmothers. She takes us through ancient history, fairy stories, the few existing research studies on the effects of divorce and, for want of any psychoanalytic literature, case studies, autobiographies and self-help books in her attempt to understand the role of stepmothers in relation to their children. Whilst the author ends by indicting current psychological theories for concentrating 'on the minutiae of the inner world whilst ignoring the outside reality', she leaves the reader with plenty to think about around the effects of divorce, women's liberation, fatherhood, the legal status of stepparents and finally the implications of 'self-interest' in our 'selfish society'. This is a stimulating and courageous book not only for psychotherapists and stepparents but also for anyone facing the prospects of divorce."

– **Dr Felicity de Zulueta**, Emeritus Consultant Psychiatrist in Psychotherapy at SLaM NHS Foundation Trust

"In her books over the last fifteen years Prophecy Coles has been exploring the unacknowledged and the hidden, whether in families or in psychoanalysis, but never more radically than in her compelling new work on stepfamilies. Building on her seminal studies of sibling relationships, the 'unremembered past' across the generations, and the place of the nurse and the nanny in both psyche and culture, Coles turns her attention to our 'new configuration of family life' and its effects on the psyche. The arc of the book ranges widely, from mythology and fairy tales to literary representations of stepfamilies as well as the social and historical changes that have affected both stepparents and stepchildren, and that form the backdrop to our current clinical practice. Her argument that our psychological theories have ignored the important role that stepparents now play in our new kinship structures does not imply that we think any less about the inner world of fantasy and the unconscious mind, rather that we give full weight to the contribution of stepparents to the structure of their stepchildren's psyche, and to the intergenerational history that stepparents will bring to their stepfamily. Coles has always blended originality of thought with clinical depth and nuance, and in this significant contribution to psychoanalytic debate on the relationship between inner and outer worlds, she brings us a compassionate and challenging new study."

– **Ann Scott**, Editor-in-Chief, *British Journal of Psychotherapy*; Senior Member, British Psychotherapy Foundation

Psychoanalytic and Psychotherapeutic Perspectives on Stepfamilies and Stepparenting

Prophecy Coles

LONDON AND NEW YORK

First published 2018
by Routledge
2 Park Square, Milton Park, Abingdon, Oxon OX14 4RN

and by Routledge
711 Third Avenue, New York, NY 10017

Routledge is an imprint of the Taylor & Francis Group, an informa business

© 2018 Prophecy Coles

The right of Prophecy Coles to be identified as author of this work has been asserted by her in accordance with sections 77 and 78 of the Copyright, Designs and Patents Act 1988.

All rights reserved. No part of this book may be reprinted or reproduced or utilised in any form or by any electronic, mechanical, or other means, now known or hereafter invented, including photocopying and recording, or in any information storage or retrieval system, without permission in writing from the publishers.

Trademark notice: Product or corporate names may be trademarks or registered trademarks, and are used only for identification and explanation without intent to infringe.

British Library Cataloguing in Publication Data
A catalogue record for this book is available from the British Library

Library of Congress Cataloging in Publication Data
A catalog record for this title has been requested.

ISBN: 978-1-138-12638-1 (hbk)
ISBN: 978-1-138-12639-8 (pbk)
ISBN: 978-1-315-64686-2 (ebk)

Typeset in Times New Roman
by Swales & Willis Ltd, Exeter, Devon, UK

For Caroline, Adam, John-Fred, Sarah, Kathy,
Sam and Nathaniel.

Contents

	Acknowledgements	viii
	Introduction	1
1	The stepmother in our fairy stories	5
2	The fairy story stepfather: where is he?	19
3	The strangely shaped footprint of women	31
4	The psychic moorings of a stepchild	45
5	No longer the fairy tale stepmother	57
6	Psychoanalytic theory and stepparents	71
7	Is stepparenting all in the mind?	83
8	The new reality?	95
9	Epilogue	109
	Index	119

Acknowledgements

In the first place I would like to thank Kate Hawes for accepting my proposal for this book and her unobtrusive support, Charles Bath for overseeing this manuscript into publication, and Louise Lubke Cuss for her detailed copy editing.

This book could not have been written without the thoughtful contributions and challenging conversations I have had with Rose Baring, Charlie Boxer, Sally Cowley, Melanie Hart, Anna Hopewell, Maggie Huntingdon-Whiteley, Lisa Ireland, Dorothy Judd, Christopher Field, Val Parker, Luc Magnenat, Mark Sainsbury, Ann Scott, Jennifer Silverstone, Kate Springford, Johnathen Sunley, Isca Wittenberg and Felicity de Zulueta. They all shared with me their different perspectives on stepparents and they will find that some of their views have been incorporated into my text. I also would like to thank those who spoke to me and who have preferred to stay anonymous. They also will find their stories woven within this text. I have been particularly indebted to my daughter-in-law Tanya Stobbs who has brought her professional editorial knowledge to this text. Finally this book could not have been written without the tireless encouragement of Walter, who has read every word, several times, and whose finer appreciation of grammatical construction I utterly rely upon.

Kind permission to reproduce her painting *Through the Wood* has been given by Alison Davies.

Introduction

The idea of writing this book arose from a casual conversation that I had with a friend. She said she wished that when she had become a stepmother, some twenty years ago, there had been a book that would have given her some idea of the difficulty of the task that lay ahead. She told me how devastated she had been when she met with the hostility of her stepchild. It was as though all norms of civilized behaviour no longer existed between them, and, like many other women who marry a man with a child, she felt 'I married this man but I did not marry his child.' She felt totally ill equipped to deal with this situation.

I was shocked by this conversation, not by the heartfelt difficulties my friend had encountered when she was a newly married bride with a stepchild, but by my lack of psychological understanding about the difficulties that stepparents and stepchildren face. I had some knowledge of the repercussions of the break-up of a marriage as I had witnessed my two brothers divorcing and saw the anguish that they and their children felt, but I had never systematically thought about the problems of stepparents and stepchildren in my therapeutic work. So when I was confronted by my friend, telling me about the difficulties that followed her marriage to a man who had been married before, it felt as though a forbidden door had been opened, and there, like Bluebeard's wife, I discovered the distressing consequences of my ignorance. Stepparenting can be a bloody battle. The sudden image of Bluebeard that came to me made me wonder whether there had been an unconscious prohibition that I should not open that door. As though there had been a cultural imperative not to think about stepparents, and stepmothers in particular. One result had been that I had assumed that stepmothers are as cruel and unkind to their stepchildren as I had learned from fairy stories.

I decided to explore how the stepmother had acquired such a bad reputation and whether she deserved it. I began in Chapter 1 with the fairy story and the archetypal wicked stepmother, who emerges out of our early oral history. These stories changed over the centuries and were expressing the subtle cultural shifts that had taken place as pre-Christian beliefs became incorporated within Christian sacred beliefs. Bettelheim (1976), in two footnotes on Cinderella in his book *The Uses of Enchantment*, suggested that originally Cinderella may have been linked to a pre-Christian Roman Vestal Virgin sitting in the ashes of the family hearth guarding the home with her wisdom. This gave way, he went on to suggest, to a later Cinderella who was associated with a symbol of an early Christian belief about ashes that were sprinkled on one's head on Ash Wednesday in recognition of Christ's death. Cinderella's wicked stepmother, death and loss and Christianity become an interesting melting pot when trying to unravel the complexity of the tale.

In Chapter 2 I turned my attention to fathers in our fairy stories who do not seem to be distinguished from stepfathers. There I discovered that men get off more lightly and seldom come to a bad end in these tales. This fact seems to be linked to the transcribers of our oral tales who were for the most part men. One example is to be found in an early tale of Hansel and Gretel, who with their parents faced starvation. This was a fate that many peasants had endured over the centuries and it is not inconceivable that in these extreme circumstances children died at the hands of their parents. But by the late eighteenth century, when the story was being printed and deemed to be a tale suitable to be read to children, this idea clashed with the emerging values of the bourgeois family. The tale becomes subtly transformed into a tale about a wicked stepmother and a wicked witch and the father is exonerated. In this way, family conflicts and tragedies are pushed outside the hallowed circle of the nuclear family and the mother remains ideal.

The realization that stepfathers scarcely appeared in our fairy stories whereas stepmothers, if they were present, were always thought of as wicked, led me in Chapter 3 into exploring early pre-Christian beliefs and their link with the fairy story. I began to wonder whether some of our negative feelings about the stepmother had been projected on to her from troubling cultural fears of women generally. Pagan tales about mythical female figures, such as the Queen of Sheba or the pre-Hellenic goddess of fertility, Hera, become denigrated over the centuries and their matriarchal power goes underground. From then on, in the Western world, women were seen as possessing a secret and subversive power that threatened to overrule men.

In this way the stepmother takes on some of the more general prejudices that have been attributed to women and her image is carried into the portrait of a fictional stepmother by the nineteenth-century novelist Elizabeth Gaskell (1810–1865). My choice, in Chapter 4, of Gaskell's novel *Wives and Daughters* was because Gaskell gave an insightful portrait into the repercussions that followed the death of a mother on a widower and his emerging adolescent daughter. It was the high maternity rate that brought the role of a stepmother into being in the first place, and here is a good example of some of the consequences. Molly, the heroine of the novel, was outraged when her father decided to marry again. And in her lament she felt as though 'the piece of solid ground on which she stood had broken from the shore, and she was drifting out to the infinite sea alone.'[1] This echoed many of the accounts I have read about the emotions children can feel when confronted by a second mother.

This literary example is I believe one of the first psychological explorations that tackles the stepmother and all the difficulties that a newly re-formed family have to confront. Nonetheless the limitations of a literary example is that it leaves one wondering what happens in real life. So in Chapter 5 I take up the experience of a non-fictional stepmother Mary-Jane Clairmont (1768–1841) and her stepdaughter, Mary Shelley née Godwin (1797–1851). Here was a stepmother who failed to behave with the imaginative sensitivity that was needed towards her motherless stepchildren and it had tragic consequences upon everyone. I also discovered that Mary's father, William Godwin, as in the Cinderella story, failed to protect his daughter from the insensitivity of his second wife.

The many psychological difficulties that Mary Shelley encountered and not least her angry despair at her father William Godwin and her husband Percy Bysshe Shelley led me in Chapter 6 to explore the way psychoanalysis has approached stepparents. I discovered another cultural censorship of fathers had taken place following Freud's exploration of the unconscious mind. Psychoanalysts began to wonder whether the fairy story might be revealing unconscious fantasies in the mind. But whose mind? At this point historians of the fairy story and psychoanalysts have parted company. The historians are interested in the social origins of these tales, and what they might be telling us of the conflicts between the rich and the poor and of those with power and those who had none. Whereas psychoanalysts have taken another route away from social psychology and into the workings of the individual mind, isolated from cultural concerns.

The limitation of such an idea is that the wisdom of some of our oral tales gets lost. It is not true that these imaginative stories were told to entertain children and therefore to psychoanalyse them as fantasies in the child's mind is to detach them from the social concerns of the story-tellers.

In Chapter 7, I tackle the psychological problems stepparents and stepchildren face. There has seemed to be little concern within psychoanalytic theory about the psychological consequences of divorce and its effect on the psyche of a child who has two sets of parents. I found the most vivid accounts of the difficulties that stepparents and their stepchildren face from autobiography, self-help books and three long-term research projects of Gorell Barnes et al. (1997), Hetherington and Kelly (2002) and Wallerstein et al. (2002).

It was tempting to end my book here by saying, alongside the self-help books and the research findings, that divorce and remarriage and stepparents and stepchildren do suffer emotional difficulties, but for the most part everyone gets over them, and stepmothers, if they behave sensitively, need no longer be feared.

The only problem was that I did not believe this to be true. I had been left with a sense, in spite of the assurances from all I had read, that divorce does do lasting hurt to our children. So in Chapter 8, I consider some of the accounts I had been given by those who had divorced and those who had been stepchildren. Their views are very different. It also became clear that an important psychological consideration when understanding the impact that stepparents had upon their stepchildren was to take account of their own generational history. There were often untold difficulties that they brought to the newly forming family. This led me to wonder why our psychological theories had ignored the possibility of a stepparent or stepchild transference in our therapeutic work. Surely they must appear from time to time? Had our profession repudiated the idea of being seen as stepparent? I was helped to develop the idea of a stepparent transference by three colleagues who were willing to share their own clinical experiences with me.

The final chapter, Chapter 9, I call an Epilogue. The reason for this is that I have been left with more general questions about the extent of divorce and stepparenting in our society and the lack of psychological interest in this 'new reality.' Why are we such a divorce-prone society? Has there been a psychological reluctance to acknowledge the pain we inflict upon ourselves and our children when we divorce? One possible answer to the ubiquity of divorce is to take up Penelope Leach's (2014) point in *Family Breakdown*, that we are living in a 'me' society. Sue Gerhardt (2017), in her essay 'The Selfish Society: The Current State of Things,' develops that idea in a slightly different direction. But both are addressing the idea that we live in a materialistic society where our values are underpinned by the individual desire for self-fulfilment at the cost of concern for the wider society. One original way of addressing such issues is in the work of Amber Jacobs (2017) who returns to the unconscious nature and problems of close relationships between men and women. This in turn may help us to engage with a new energy in understanding the wider psychological task of stepparenting.

Note

1 Gaskell (1996 [1866]) p. 111.

Bibliography

Bettelheim, B. (1976) *The Uses of Enchantment*. Harmondsworth: Penguin Books Ltd.
Gaskell, E. (1996 [1866]) *Wives and Daughters*. London: Penguin Books.
Gerhardt, S. (2017) The Selfish Society: The Current State of Things. In *The Political Self: Understanding the Social Context for Mental Illness*. Ed R. Tweedy. London: Karnac Books Ltd.
Gorell Barnes, G., Thompson, T., Daniel, G. and Burchardt, N. (1998) *Growing Up in Stepfamilies*. Oxford: Clarendon Press.
Hetherington, E.M. and Kelly, J. (2002) *For Better of for Worse: Divorce Reconsidered*. New York/ London: W.W. Norton & Co.
Jacobs, A. (2017) Rethinking Matricide. In *The Mother in Psychoanalysis and Beyond*. Ed. R. Mayo and C. Moutsou. London: New York: Routledge.
Leach, P. (2014) *Family Breakdown*. London: Unbound.
Wallerstein, J., Lewis, J. and Blakeslee, S. (2002) *The Unexpected Legacy of Divorce: A 25 Year Landmark Study*. London: Fusion Press.

Chapter 1

The stepmother in our fairy stories

> Little brother took his little sister by the hand and said 'Since our mother died we have had no happiness; our stepmother beats us every day, and if we come near her she kicks us away with her foot. Our meals are hard crusts of bread that are left over; and the little dog under the table is better off, for she often throws it a choice morsel. God pity us, if only our mother knew! Come we will go forth together into the wide world' . . . But the wicked step-mother, because of whom the children had gone out into the world, had never thought but that the sister had been torn to pieces by the wild beasts in the wood, and that the brother had been shot for a roebuck by the huntsman. Now when she heard that they were so happy, and so well off, envy and jealousy rose in her heart and left her no peace, and she thought of nothing but how she could again bring them to misfortune.[1]

This Grimm story encapsulates the prejudiced image we all have of the stepmother. She is of a jealous and envious disposition and she wishes to get rid of her stepchildren so that her own children can flourish. In the fairy story above she has one 'ugly' daughter who is equally envious. However, as in all the best fairy stories, the brother and sister survive and the stepmother and her daughter come to a gruesome end.

> The King ordered both to be led before the judge, and judgment was delivered against them. The daughter was taken into the forest where she was torn to pieces by wild beasts, but the witch [stepmother] was cast into the fire and miserably burned.[2]

I was prompted to write this book because I realized that as a psychotherapist I had never listened to any of my clients with the question in my mind as to whether their difficulties had links with being a stepmother or a stepchild. So how was I to write a book about stepparents without my own clinical material? The right place to begin seemed to be with the fairy stories that contain a stepmother, and that set me wondering not only whether stepmothers in reality are as wicked as in our tales, but if they are not, then what are these stories about wicked stepmothers about? What are they telling us?

As I have pursued these questions I have relied on the scholarship of Jack Zipes[3] and Marina Warner.[4] They have taken me on roads that I would have never ventured down and from them I have been helped to imagine something of the ancestral history of our fables and the place the stepmother has had in them. Zipes has suggested that the fairy story emerges out of oral tales that have stretched back thousands of years across the world and the basic form of these tales has been about human social and emotional conflict.[5] These fables and legends were not told by sophisticated and well-educated people; on the contrary, they were tales that were told by pre-literate people as they grappled with superstitious beliefs, rituals and the need to hold their community together co-operatively. These tales describe the puzzling phenomenon of the natural world, whether a terrifying encounter with strange and powerful animals or natural storms and disasters; they portray conflict within society and the family and they approach, by subtle means, the inherent difficulties that the underprivileged encounter in the face of power and wealth.[6] The subversive element of the fairy story is often disguised as though it was an innocent story about animals or insects, as in the fables of Aesop.[7] One of our best-known fairy stories, Beauty and the Beast, it has been claimed, was originally an oral tale that grew from ancient pagan fertility rites, in which young men and women may have been sacrificed to appease the anger of a fabled creature or god.[8]

I came to realize that human suffering and the heroic and imaginative narratives that are created to depict and criticize social reality are inextricably intertwined. The power that our fairy stories retain to this day is that they can stir up passionate feelings in the reader about injustice and inequality, while at the same time, help us to imagine that we could change the way things are. They touch our dreams of a utopia where goodness will overcome evil; the rich will be overthrown; the peasant's wisdom will prevail and the witch and the wicked stepmother will come to a fitting end as they fall into a cauldron of boiling water.

If there is a hidden theme in our folk tales, the difficult question will be to try and understand why the stepmother always needs to come to a bad end.

The stepmother has not been of much interest to some who have researched the origins and meanings of these tales. For instance, a nineteenth-century researcher into many variants of the Cinderella fairy story remarked, 'The stepmother opening of the story is too simple to require an explanation.'[9] But is that the case? Is she no more than part of the cultural architecture of the fairy story? And should she be ignored without explanation? Both Zipes and Warner have in their different ways commented upon this lack of interest. Zipes asks, 'Why is the stepmother shown to be wicked and not the father, who abandons and neglects his daughter?' And then he adds, 'How difficult is it for the young girl to accept the role of step-daughter or to accept a "new" stepmother? Conversely, how difficult is it for the stepmother to accept her husband's daughter when she has two daughters of her own?'[10] For Warner, there is an imperative need to tackle the prejudice against the stepmother for, 'As remarriage becomes more and more common, stepmothers find they are tackling a hard crust of bigotry set in the minds of their new children, and refreshed by endless returns of the wicked stepmother in the literature of childhood.'[11]

One explanation of why the stepmother is seen in such a negative light can be linked to her definition. The word 'stepmother,' in the *Shorter Oxford Dictionary*, is said to derive from the Middle English word *seif*, that in turn was associated with 'bereaved,' most commonly used to describe an 'orphan,' and over time the stepmother came to denote the mother of a bereaved child.[12] It follows from this definition, whether in a fairy story or in real life, that she is not the proper mother; she is merely stepping into the shoes of a dead mother and we must never forget that she is no more than a replacement or 'second mother.'[13] Once we can see that her very existence is predicated upon maternal loss the prejudices against her become more understandable. But as a 'second mother' she has important differences with other 'second mothers,' such as the nanny or wet nurse. It is these differences that are quite complicated to unravel. The wet nurse or nanny, who though she nurtured the rich and the poor throughout recorded history, has always found herself in a small corner of interest in our social history and biography. Indeed, until quite recently, she was not considered to have had any important influence upon the psychological development of the child, and so she has seldom featured in our recorded history. By contrast the stepmother, who is also a 'second mother,' shouts loudly at us in our fairy stories, printing indelibly in our minds that she is wicked and not to be trusted.

One reason for this difference is that the stepmother is imprisoned by the definition that she is a 'step' mother. She is not only standing in the shoes of a dead mother but, paradoxically, there is a social and cultural imperative that she should not be seen as better than the mother. By way of contrast the wet nurse or nanny, who in many cases takes the place of the mother in the early years of a child's life, never receives the same social prejudice. If you were not a good wet nurse the child would die and you might lose your professional status, therefore it was incumbent on you to be a good one. The stepmother has always brought with her a more complicated history to the nurturing of another woman's child. Her role is not predicated upon being a good stepmother. Once she has managed to marry a widower who would provide for her, she does not depend upon being good at the job of looking after other people's children. One consequence has been that this 'second mother' has been seen as lacking proper maternal care, while at the same time she has often contributed to her own bad reputation. There have of course been some stepmothers who have been good, but the stepmother has always battled against a visceral feeling that we do not like her; and in our imagination we associate her with the unkind stepmother as in the fairy story of Cinderella.

The unravelling of the ubiquitous image of the stepmother who is not to be trusted is to be found across the history of the family and in imaginative fiction. In the fairy story her most enduring image in our minds is the stepmother in Cinderella.

It is believed that the original tale of Cinderella comes from the ninth century AD in China.[14] In this tale Cinderella does not have a stepmother, as we know it, but she suffers under the hands of her father's 'other' wife when her mother dies. She is the daughter of a polygamous marriage, which was a unique part of the family structure in China at the time. It is worth noting that in this early version Cinderella only has one stepsister who does not play a major role in her unhappiness. What is common in this tale, as in all the other Cinderella stories, is that Cinderella has a small foot and only one shoe will fit it. This small foot leads to the final discovery of her true identity. In China the female foot was seen as the symbol of beauty and sexual power from the time of the Tang Dynasty (AD 618–907) when foot binding was the mark of aristocracy and true worth. So it is tempting to imagine that this earliest Chinese tale spread along the Silk Route, as merchants were trading and entertaining each other at resting posts, and it was in this way that the symbolism of the shoe tucked itself into the European mind and got taken up in later legends.[15] Be that as it may, the universal feature of the size of Cinderella's foot seems to confirm Freud's suggestion that the foot can become a fetishized symbol of the female genitals.[16]

This idea has found general agreement amongst historians of the fairy story, and so it seems safe to say that a central aspect of the Cinderella story concerns a young woman's potential fertility that arouses an older woman's sexual jealousy. But that does not mean that the jealousy of an older woman for a younger woman's beauty and sexuality is necessarily aroused because the older woman is a stepmother. It is true that in all the known versions of the Cinderella tale, East and West, Cinderella suffers in the hands of a wicked stepmother. However in other tales, such as Hansel and Gretel or Snow White, the Grimm Brothers changed the mother into the stepmother, which does suggest that oral legends undergo change as they are written down and published and that the stepmother can be used to conceal the more controversial image of an unkind or jealous mother, in order to preserve an idealized image of motherhood.[17]

In spite of this more general question as to whether the stepmother might sometimes have 'stepped' in to preserve the image of the good mother, the stepmother is always represented as cruel in the many versions of the Cinderella tale that have come down to us, while other details about her life have changed. In the Chinese Cinderella the stepmother was already there in the family as a concubine, so she did not enter as a stranger, unlike the Western versions. A more important cultural detail in the Chinese Cinderella concerns the fate of the stepmother and her daughter when their envious jealousy is discovered. They are first of all stoned to death, but over time their violent end evokes pity and the moral ending of the tale is not that they vanish and nothing more is known about them, but their graves become 'The Tomb of Regretful Women' and they become 'the goddesses of match-makers.' However this change is believed to be 'an intrusion of a legendary nature and is irrelevant to the story.'[18] Whatever the truth may be as to whether this ending is added on later or not, it reminds us of the changing nature of these tales and the way in which the tellers of the tale often subject the story to the values of the society in which the tale is being told.

It might be said that this change suggests that the Chinese are more sympathetic or understanding towards the stepmother, in contrast to later European versions in which she always remains as an evil force. But even if our versions always depict the stepmother in a negative way, a shift does takes place in the relationship that she has with her stepdaughter, as the Western tale is retold. There are early versions of the tale in which Cinderella is not pictured as the passive blonde princess whose unfailing goodness outweighs the evil and envious machinations of her wicked stepmother, as it has come down to us today; instead Cinderella and her stepmother have a much more confrontational relationship.[19]

One of the first European transcriptions of Cinderella was printed in 1634–1636 by the Italian Giambattista Basile (1575–1632). It was called *The Cat Cinderella (La Gatta Cennerentola)*.[20] Basile was living in Naples and he was interested in collecting the tales he heard around him told him by old women in their native dialect. In this tale Cinderella is called Zezolla. Her mother has died and she suffers at the hands of her stepmother but she has a governess who treats her well. One day her governess suggests that if Zezolla kills her stepmother, she, the governess, will marry Zezolla's father and they will all live as a happy family. Encouraged by her governess Zezolla succeeds in killing her stepmother by banging a trunk lid onto her head and breaking her neck. However the governess proves to be no kinder to Zezolla than her previous stepmother and she treats Zezolla with contempt and cruelty and Zezolla ends up as a kitchen maid. Furthermore the governess brings in her own children which adds to the weight of Zezolla's displaced position. Zezolla finally escapes her dreary life as a servant and with the help of fairies and a date tree she finds a king for a husband.

What is unique in this tale is Zezolla's violence towards her first stepmother. Here we have a robust Cinderella in which she is murderously angry about the cruel treatment by her stepmother and then her governess. This version of Cinderella, that Basile had probably taken from the fourteenth-century Arthurian romance, *Perceforest*, has never been popularized, and like many other energetic and vital and violent folk tales, it has been sidelined and largely forgotten.[21] It is hard to imagine that a Disney film of Zezolla would fulfil the American Dream and fill the box office. But in toning down Cinderella's anger some of her vitality is lost and the energy of the tale gets directed or projected onto the stepmother. This noticeable shift away from Cinderella's vitality and rage reflects the changing social values of female virtue over the centuries, so that by the time the Grimm Brothers in the nineteenth century have refashioned the tale, the ideal of female attractiveness has become much more passive, and Cinderella can no longer challenge her fate. But the energy of the tale has to go somewhere, so purloining a combustible Freudian idea, the stepmother becomes the vehicle of this energy and becomes even more powerful.[22]

There is another interesting development in the details of the Cinderella tale that can be seen when comparing the small part that the stepsister has in the ninth-century Chinese Cinderella with later European versions. In the Western Cinderella there are two stepsisters and they hold a more significant place as the tale unfolds. In the early seventeenth-century version collected by Perrault (1628–1703) he treats them quite lightly and they are not sadistically punished for their jealousy. Instead and in spite of their mutilated feet they are given respectable courtiers to marry so that they could live alongside Cinderella, duly penitent one hopes. One reason for Perrault's light touch was that he was part of the Court of Louis XIV, and the ruffles of the courtiers were not to be too disturbed by his tales, especially those of the ladies of the court for whom he was writing. He therefore implied that unruly jealousy between women was no more than a passing phase and the 'ugly sisters' did not come to a painful end.

By contrast the Grimm Brothers in the early nineteenth century describe a stepmother who encourages her daughters, or the 'ugly sisters,' to mock and deride Cinderella and treat her as a servant. Later the stepmother desperately wishes her daughters might succeed in challenging their stepsister's sexual attractiveness. What is interesting in the Grimms' account is that the final retribution for the 'ugly sisters,' at Cinderella's wedding, is that their eyes are plucked out. This focusing upon the sibling relationships reflects the values of the Grimm Brothers and the audience for whom they were writing. They were writing for a German audience concerned with upholding the values of the Protestant bourgeois family and in which jealousy between siblings was considered reprehensible and should be harshly treated. From this point of view it was quite fitting that at the end of the tale the 'ugly sisters'' eyes should be plucked out.[23]

Where does this take us in our understanding of why the stepmother, in spite of all these changes of emphasis, always remains the same, wicked and revengeful? This is where real life and our fairy stories get entwined and it becomes difficult to distinguish between the fantasy stepmother and her presence in the world. One way of thinking about the stepmother has been to see her as the split image of the real mother. The real mother is both loved and hated but because we find that difficult to accept, our hatred of her is projected onto the stepmother. The problem with this psychological view is that it loses sight of the social reality in which our oral tales are embedded and it has the effect of dismissing the stepmother as a significant figure in the child's life. The origin of the fairy story about Cinderella was not describing fantasies in the mind but was a tale that was grounded in the tragic effect upon a child when a mother dies and a stepmother takes over. A stepmother does not embody a projected fantasy of maternal ambivalence but needs to be understood as a real presence in the life of a child. For instance the high maternal mortality rates up until the late nineteenth century meant that one mother in four died in childbirth with the result that 'a stepmother in the household . . . came perilously close to counting as the rule than as an exception.'[24]

In a family where the mother dies the father will usually marry again. Historically this has meant that many men will have had at least two wives and many children will have had several mothers.[25] It is therefore not hard to imagine that some of the hatred that the stepmother acquired must reflect the feelings that many children who lost their mother will have had. When they grow up and become the tellers of the tale and re-visit the loss of their own mother, their story will gain dramatic strength by emphasizing a fantasy of a lost paradise that had been rudely intruded upon by a wicked interloper. In other words, the stepmother, quite apart from whether she was good or bad, came to represent the fantasy that until she came along, family life was harmonious and happy.

Another problem stepmothers have faced in the real world has been attached to a belief, or was it no more than a hope, that a stepmother could be a seamless substitute for a natural mother. There was a belief that dominated European child-rearing practices up until the eighteenth century that infants did not notice who was looking after them so they could be handed over to wet nurses or nannies and suffer no ill effects.[26] The fairy story, and Cinderella's tale in particular, confronts this false belief and the painful truth is that Cinderella does mind what happens to her. Her stepmother is a bad mother and this confronts the delusional hope that any mother can bring up another person's child because the child will not notice the difference.[27] But there is another difficulty the stepmother faces and this is especially true in the case of a stepmother who brings her own children into the family. Cinderella's stepmother demotes Cinderella to the role of a servant and the lives of her own daughters are promoted. In this way the stepmother threatens the very heart of the natural order of inheritance. Inheritance was one of the foundation stones of medieval family life, and once a stepmother challenges this natural order by pushing her own children forward, the way is open for superstitious fears to creep in.[28] She can become linked in fantasy to an unnatural old crone or an ancient woman on a broom-stick, who threatens the very foundation stones of orderly society and the family. And so we see a stepmother is always battling with a deeply held superstition that she is unnatural, or to put it into twenty-first-century psychological language, there is no biological attachment between a stepmother and her stepchild, which is what makes their relationship so fraught with mis-attunement.[29]

When Cinderella's stepmother attempts to promote her own children over the natural inheritance of Cinderella, as the eldest child, her behaviour is highlighting another real life problem that a widow with children faced. All too often she could find herself homeless and without means.[30] It is not hard to imagine that Cinderella's stepmother was desperate not only to find a husband who would look after her, but also to secure a satisfactory future for her children. We could understand that when she tells her two daughters to mutilate their feet so that the slipper would fit one or other of them, this is a desperate symbolic enactment of a widow prepared to do anything for her fatherless children. Her frenzy to advance her own children could not be better described as she encourages them to cut their feet into an acceptable shape, and at this painful moment, the tale leans towards a raw appreciation of the problem of 'stepping' into another family with one's own children.

There has been another significant problem of inheritance that widows who became stepmothers faced when they became part of a new family. Women have always lived longer than men and so there have always been more widows than widowers, or one could say that there have never been enough men to go around.

What is also true, for rich and poor, is that throughout history men have married later than women; men might be in their mid-twenties but their wives would be young girls in their late teens. Until the nineteenth century the average length of marriage was about fourteen years, so what happened to these young women when their husbands died?[31] In most cases they would have children and therefore they would be looking for another husband to support them. But these young widows would be feared as they would be seen as rivals by younger unmarried girls who were also looking for partners. It is therefore not surprising to discover that these widows were hated because they were in danger of taking away a putative husband from a young girl. Another way of putting it was that a widow who was looking for a second husband was seen as a sexual predator by her society, and this is well reflected in the Cinderella tale.

If the Cinderella tale reflects a complex mix of real life family problems, social values and superstitious fantasies in the face of ever-present death, something even more telling happens to the stepmother with the development of printing and the gradual popularization of the fairy story by the end of the seventeenth century. The image of the stepmother becomes firmly fixed in the imagination as she is folded into the printed pages of a fairy story and she takes on the role of an archetype. In the early Disney *Cinderella* he reinforces this belief when he portrays her with witch-like characteristics, and Cinderella undergoes a similar though benign transformation; she becomes the passive and beautiful blonde princess, who is dressed in blue. The *Shorter Oxford Dictionary* defines archetype as being constituted by nature and so we see that both stepmother and stepdaughter become defined by their nature. Cinderella gives up her rage and becomes a saintly princess and the stepmother, once she is locked onto the printed page, becomes tightly screwed into the position of a destructive woman. It is hard not to agree with Kenneth Clarke's (1969) ironic remark that 'people used to think of the invention of printing as the lynchpin in the history of civilization ... fifth-century Greece, and twelfth-century Chartres and early fifteenth-century Florence got on very well without it.'[32] And we might add so did the folk tale, and especially the stepmother, get along better without being confined within the pages of a book.

There is one final point that needs to be added to our archetypal image of the stepmother. This has sprung from a philological confusion between stepmother and mother-in-law. In many languages the role of stepmother and mother-in-law have not been distinguished. In France *belle mère* and *belle soeur* are still used interchangeably between mother-in-law and sister-in-law and stepmother and stepsister, as was true in English until the nineteenth century.[33] One of the earliest tales about a supposed wicked stepmother was in fact about a future mother-in-law. This was the tale of Cupid and Psyche as told by Apuleius (AD 140–185) in *The Golden Ass.* The so-called stepmother was Venus, who was jealous of the beauty of Psyche and did all in her power to get rid of her so that her precious son Cupid would not marry her. So it can be seen from this folk legend that the stepmother has had added to her negative image that of the role of a jealous mother-in-law and this has fuelled our emotionally complicated image of the stepmother.

There remains one interesting puzzle about the character of the stepmother. Warner raises a question: who were the narrators of our folk tales? As we have already seen, the story-tellers were often mocked and their stories were seen as no more than 'old wives' tales.' Many of these ancient stories were told by women, who may have been grandmothers, or nurses and nannies, or women who spent their days spinning and weaving, and if that was the case, why would a woman want to tell tales about destructive envy and jealousy between women?[34] Such a portrayal would put women in a bad light and give substance to male misogyny. In trying to unravel that question, we plunge into further layers of social history that are embedded in our fairy stories, at the same time as opening up new ways of thinking about women's history of themselves.

If we imagine that the teller of the tale of Cinderella was a mother-in-law, then she might be warning young girls of the trials they may suffer at her hands when they marry and have to go and live with their husband's family. The message may have been 'expect to be badly treated in your new home by your mother-in-law until you have proved your worth. I know because I have been both a young bride and a mother-in-law myself.' Understood in this way the tale may be giving comfort and a sense of female solidarity across the generations. Warner argues this point very convincingly by taking into consideration the conditions of marriage for young women. They would often be married at a young age, and be sent off to the family of their prospective husband and may never have seen their own family again.[35]

If we imagine that Cinderella herself may be telling the tale from the vantage point of being an old woman, she could be telling young girls what it feels like to lose a mother and gain an unwelcomed stepmother. From such a perspective the tale might be read as a subtle tale of revenge upon the stepmother for treating her stepdaughter so badly. This is a much more robust Cinderella, as teller of the tale, who exacts a most appealing retribution upon the stepmother and the tormenting 'ugly sisters.' She may be saying to her listeners, who are suffering under the hands of powerful women, 'the time will come when you will be able to get your own revenge.'

Finally, perhaps the woman telling the tale against the stepmother may have been voicing a visceral prejudice that women have against other women taking the place of the mother. This may sound paradoxical in the face of the child-rearing practices that I referred to above. Until the late eighteenth century it was quite common amongst the privileged middle class to send their children away from home into the country to be brought up by wet nurses. This would suggest that many mothers did not value the early mother and child relationship in the way we do today. Other less fortunate women who had had an illegitimate child or were in extreme poverty were often forced to abandon their children in church porches, or foundling hospitals or on the streets. Reading accounts of what these women felt, whether in the Verney diaries or in the notes that were pinned to the children at the London Foundling Hospital, these women suffered.[36] They hoped that their children would be loved and well looked after. But there was to be found in the hearts of many of these women a deep anxiety that another woman, who was not the mother of their child, might not be reliable and trustworthy. It was this anxiety that could be personified in the image of the stepmother and she became the emblem of this suspicion.

Where do these ideas about the stepmother lead? Why does the stepmother, in spite of the enormous social changes in beliefs and ideas, both in the real world and in the way the fairy story has been recorded, nevertheless remain reviled over nearly two centuries of story-telling? We have seen the way the imaginative forces of the fairy story get intermingled with the social conditions under which the story is told. In the Zezolla story, value is given to Zezolla having a mind of her own. By the time the Cinderella tale is being retold by the Grimm Brothers, very different societal pressures were at work. There was a significant shift in values about the family and children were beginning to be seen in new ways and the early folk tales were being trimmed into fairy stories that were suitable for them. This meant that Cinderella, in the hands of the Grimm Brothers, becomes 'a particular kind of social engineering with strong political overtones ... the children against the evil witch, the wicked stepmother, pretending to be kind.'[37]

The stepmother has had a fraught and difficult history. In many tales in which she is featured she can be seen to reflect real experiences. Gregory of Tours (538–594) told the story of a sixth-century Queen Fredegund, 'who was a living example of the vilest step-mother ever imagined in the pages of a fairy-book.'[38] So the prejudice against the stepmother, as in the Cinderella tale, lies in some respects in the reality of the past in which she played a part in the cruelty and suffering of family life. She is also a reminder of the fact that we are all dependent upon a mother for our life, with all the ambivalent feelings we have about her.[39] This last point has been hard to imagine, culturally and emotionally and as we have seen, some transcribers of our fairy stories, such as the Grimm Brothers, have shifted negative feelings away from the mother onto the stepmother. But that is not all, as I shall explore in Chapter 3. The gradual shift in beliefs away from the earlier pre-literate matriarchal origins of society, to the reasoned beliefs of patriarchal order, has meant that women have gone underground, as it were, and have found a way of continuing to knit together a meaningful social fabric to their lives by gossiping and telling tales about the injustices of power. They can tell alarming tales that frighten men into asking 'What do women desire?' But it is not only men that have been frightened of women's power. If we imagine that women sometimes told the tale, women may have been issuing a warning about women who step into the shoes of the absent, abandoning or dead mother.

I was drawn to such a thought when I read about a fairy story that was being told in 1958 in French Dahomey. The narrator of the tale was a young child whose mother had died. He was suffering under the hands of a stepmother until one day the mother visited the stepmother from the grave and struck her dead! The narrator ends the tale by saying, 'One never mistreats orphans. For once you mistreat them you die. You die the same day. You are not even sick. I know that myself, I am an orphan.' This was drawing attention to the idea that if you do not look after your stepchild well you will come to an unnatural end. Perhaps that idea could be extended to the Cinderella tale, and all other fairy stories that have a stepmother, and this might help us to see that what makes the Cinderella story so powerful today is the exhortation that 'a second wife must look after the dead women's child better than after her own children' or else![40]

This modern fairy story takes one back to one constant thread that the stepmother can never escape: she is a reminder of the loss of the mother, for whatever reason. The power and one might say the truth of the fairy story with a wicked stepmother is that it helps us all to understand that when a mother dies, or in our contemporary life, when she divorces or is divorced, everyone has a hard time; the children, the stepmother and her stepchildren, as well as the father. In other words such a fairy story as Cinderella illuminates some of the social as well as psychological conflicts that follow on from the tragic displacement of a mother; but it does not follow that the stepmother is by nature wicked.

In conclusion, when I began to think about the lack of psychological interest in the stepmother as a real person in the real lives of families, I was at the same time confronted with a cultural stereotype that she was wicked. The idea that she was essentially destructive seemed to have grown out of our fairy stories that have been part of our imaginative culture; and this image of her has been reinforced once these tales were collected and written down by the mid-seventeenth century. She is a hated reminder of the tragic and disruptive forces to family life that follow on from maternal death and as a result she haunts our fairy stories as though she was an emblem of destruction. This image of her has been reinforced by medieval beliefs about witches and ancient crones who cast evil spells upon their unfortunate victims. But while such fantasy images of her resonate in our imagination it also leads to the realization that our beliefs about her are inescapably part of the history of the values of the societies in which these tales are told. The contrast between the way stepmothers are described in Charles Perrault's fairy stories with those of the Grimm Brothers shows the way shifts in values about the family bring about changes in the tale.

The stepmother in our fairy stories, though she has been lamentably short of maternal concern for her stepchildren, has accumulated a history of attrition that has made it difficult to think about her except as a negative and destructive force who brings harm to the family. This has encouraged children to have 'a hard crust of bigotry'[41] about her, as Warner warned, adding to the difficulties that many families face today as marriages fall apart and second mothers have to be accommodated. I hope that this exploration of the nature of the fairy story may lead to a further understanding of why the stepmother continues to this day to be seen as a person who needs to be feared. This myth needs challenging, even if there is evidence that she has at times lived up to our cultural stereotype. Only in this way might we hope that we can get a better perspective on the psychological effects of having a stepmother.

Notes

1. Grimm (2004) p. 48.
2. Grimm (2004) 'Brother and Sister' (pp. 48–53).
3. Zipes (1979, 2002, 2012).
4. Warner (1995, 2014).
5. Zipes (1979).
6. Zipes (1979).
7. For instance, Aesop's fables 'were short and primarily featured animals, which were anthropomorphized and exemplified a moral' (Zipes 2012 p. 10).
8. Zipes (1979).
9. Ralston (1982) p. 52.
10. Zipes (1979) p. 195.
11. Warner (2014) p. 124.
12. Schectman (1993): 'In fairy tales she arrives in the face of death, summoned by the family's loss' (pp. xv–xvi).
13. 'there have always been political, social, economic and psychological reasons that have accompanied the employment of a 'second mother,' and in many cases they have clashed with the 'ideal of the sacred duties of parents' (Coles 2015 p. 122).
14. Jameson (1982).
15. In the sixteenth century '[t]he influence of the Silk Roads began to be felt in the arts' (Frankopan 2015 p. 256).
16. Freud (1916–1917 p. 158) '*Shoes* and *slippers* are female genitals.' See also Warner (1995) on 'women's hidden nether parts' (p. 128) such as the webbed footed Mother Goose and the cloven hoofed Queen of Sheba and their associations to female sexuality.
17. 'Cinderella's wish to eliminate Mother is completely repressed in the modern versions and replaced by a displacement and a projection: it is not Mother who overtly plays a crucial role in the girl's life, but a stepmother' (Bettelheim 1976 p. 249). Also, Warner (1995) 'The Grimm Brothers . . . softened the harshness . . . in Hansel and Gretel . . . and turned the mother into a wicked stepmother' (p. 211).
18. Jameson (1982) pp. 77–79.
19. An Armenian Cinderella tells of two older sisters who eat their mother (Philip 1989).
20. Dundes (1982) pp. 3–14.
21. Warner (2014) p. 220.
22. Freud (1933).
23. 'The Grimm brothers . . . received strict religious training in the Reform Calvinist Church' (Zipes 2002 p. 3).
24. Stone (1990) p. 48.
25. See Stone (1990) on the change in family structure and values by the end of the sixteenth century. See also *Oxford Shorter Dictionary* on the stepmother, 'said of a bird that hatches another bird's eggs (1567).'
26. See Coles (2015) on the 'second mother.'
27. It is interesting to consider whether there is a similar belief for parents who adopt children. I am indebted to Tanya Stobbs for raising that question.
28. See Stone (1990), Fildes (1988) and Klapisch-Zuber (1987) on inheritance.
29. Stern (1985).
30. Le Roy Ladurie (1978): In medieval France, 'Marriages usually came to an end through the death of one of the partners, usually the man' (p. 200) and Stone (1990), 'The expectation of life at birth in England in the 1640s was only 32 years' (p. 55).
31. Fildes (1988), Stone (1990).
32. Clarke (1971 p. 45).
33. Warner (1995 p. 218).
34. Warner (1995 pp. 13–14).

35 Stone (1990), Warner (1995).
36 Boswell (1988), Coles (2015) and Fildes (1988).
37 McGregor (2014 p. 56).
38 Dundes (1982 p. 12).
39 Parker (1995).
40 Warner (1995) p. 214.
41 Warner (1995) p. 237.

References

Apuleius, L. (1930 [1556]) *The Golden Ass*. Trans. W. Aldington. Abbey Classics. London: Simpkin Marshall Ltd.
Bettelheim, B. (1976) *The Uses of Enchantment: The Meaning and Importance of Fairy Tales*. London: Penguin Books.
Boswell, J. (1988) *The Kindness of Strangers: The Abandonment of Children in Western Europe from Later Antiquity to the Renaissance*. London: Penguin.
Clarke, K. (1971) *Civilisation: A Personal View*. London: British Broadcasting Corporation and John Murray.
Coles, P. (2015) *The Shadow of the Second Mother: Nurses and Nannies in Theories of Infant Development*. London/New York: Routledge.
Dundes, A. Ed. (1982) *Cinderella: A Casebook*. London/Wisconsin: University of Wisconsin Press.
Fildes, V. (1988) *Wet Nursing: A History from Antiquity to the Present*. Oxford: Basil Blackwell.
Frankopan, P. (2015) *The Silk Road: A New History of the World*. London: New York: Bloomsbury.
Freud, S. (1916–1917) Introductory Lectures on Psychoanalysis. In *The Standard Edition of the Complete Psychological Works of Sigmund Freud. Vol. 15–16*. London: Hogarth Press.
Freud, S. (1933) New Introductory Lectures on Psychoanalysis. In *The Standard Edition of the Complete Psychological Works of Sigmund Freud. Vol. XXI*. London: Hogarth Press.
Grimm, J and W. (2004) *Complete Fairy Tales*. London/New York: Routledge & Kegan Paul.
Jameson, R.D. (1982) Cinderella in China. In *Cinderella: A Casebook*. Ed. A. Dundes. London/Wisconsin: University of Wisconsin Press.
Klapisch-Zuber, C. (1987) *Women, Family and Ritual in Renaissance Italy*. Chicago/London: Chicago University Press.
Le Roy Ladurie, E. (1978) *Montaillou: The World-Famous Portrait of Life in a Medieval Village*. Trans. B. Bray. London: Penguin Books Ltd.
McGregor, N. (2014) *Germany: Memories of a Nation*. London: Allen Lane/Penguin Books.
Perrault. C. (2009) *The Complete Fairy Tales*. Trans C. Betts. Oxford: Oxford University Press.
Parker, R. (1995) *Mother Love Mother Hate: The Power of Maternal Ambivalence*. London: Basic Books.
Philip, N. (1989) *The Cinderella Story*. London: Penguin Books.
Ralston, W.R.S. (1982) Cinderella. In *Cinderella: A Casebook*. Ed. A. Dundes. London/Wisconsin: University of Wisconsin Press.

Schectman, J. (1993) *The Stepmother in Fairy Tales: Bereavement and the Feminine Shadow*. Boston: Sigo Press.

Shorter Oxford English Dictionary (1972) Oxford: Oxford University Press.

Stern, D.N. (1985) *The Interpersonal World of the Child: A View from Psychoanalysis and Development Psychology*. New York: Basic Books.

Stone, L. (1990) *The Family, Sex and Marriage in England 1500–1800* (abridged). London: Penguin Books.

Tatar, M. (2003) *The Hard Facts of the Grimms' Fairy Tales*. Princeton/Woodstock: Princeton University Press.

Warner, M. (1995) *From the Beast to the Blonde: On Fairy Tales and Their Tellers*. London: Vintage Books.

Warner, M. (2014) *Once Upon a Time: A Short History of Fairy Tale*. Oxford: Oxford University Press.

Zipes, J. (1979) *Breaking the Magic Spell: Radical Theories of Folk and Fairy Tales*. Kentucky: University Press of Kentucky.

Zipes, J. (2002) *The Brothers Grimm: From Enchanted Forests to the Modern World*. New York/ Basingstoke: Palgrave Macmillan.

Zipes, J. (2012) *The Irresistible Fairy Tale: The Cultural and Social History of a Genre*. Princeton/Woodstock: Princeton University Press.

Chapter 2

The fairy story stepfather
Where is he?

We have no enduring archetypal image of the fairy story stepfather in contrast to the images we have of the fairy story stepmother. We have no idea if he is always believed to be unkind; furthermore on the few occasions when he is mentioned we are never led to expect that he has hidden supernatural or magical powers that might change a life with a wave of a magic wand. In Warner's (1995) comprehensive book about fairy stories the stepfather does not even have an entry in the index and I have only been able to find four tales in which he is mentioned.[1] In these four tales that do mention him, there is another striking fact: he never comes to an unfortunate end, in contrast to the wicked stepmother. He seems to fade out of the tale and he certainly never suffers any retribution. This division or split between the way stepmothers and stepfathers are depicted in our fairy stories does give rise to the question, as Bettelheim (1976) asked, why is it as rare to find a bad stepfather in fairy stories as it is frequent to find an evil stepmother?[2] Zipes (1979) rephrased the question in a slightly different way, 'Why is the stepmother shown to be wicked and not the father, who abandons and neglects his daughter?'[3]

One answer is that fathers and stepfathers have throughout history played a much less significant role in child rearing during the early years of infancy. Until the nineteenth century the only chance of survival depended upon the newborn child being fed with 'mother's milk,' and so the maternal figure was necessarily all important.[4] Yet, due to the high mortality rate of mothers, following childbirth, and the short life span of men, there were few families where both couples survived for a lifetime. Stone (1990) suggested that between 1500 and 1800 in the UK, 'Perhaps a quarter of all families' were composed of widows and widowers with stepchildren of their own,[5] and the life expectancy of both partners in a marriage might last no more than fourteen years.[6]

The puzzle is that if the fairy tale is entwined with real events in the real world, as I believe it is, one might have expected to find some wicked or unkind fathers and stepfathers somewhere in these tales. So why are they seldom represented? It seems that though fathers have never played an essential part in early infant care and upbringing, there has also been a cultural censorship that took place as our oral tales were collected, in the early eighteenth and nineteenth century. They had to be refashioned into tales that would not disturb the sensibilities of the growing and educated middle classes in Europe and England and at the same time they became fairy stories that were suitable to be told to children. The dominating ethos of the time upheld the belief that masculine authority was necessary in order to hold back the tide of women's irrational moods. What children needed to know was that the machinations of old women, who cast wicked spells, could be counteracted by charming princes who could break them. They also needed to know that if men behaved irrationally, they were temporarily under the influence of the devil, and, this was the crucial point, this did not change their honourable masculine character as their behaviour had merely been a moment of madness.[7]

What is also interesting about stepfathers in contrast to stepmothers is that they were not distinguished from fathers. They both fell under the rubric of 'father,' so a 'father' may in fact be referring to a 'stepfather,' and I shall do the same in all that follows and not necessarily distinguish between them. The reason for this lack of distinction is that the father figure has had a much less ambiguous place in our cultural imagination, and therefore there has been less of a psychological need to project his worst characteristics onto another, namely the stepfather. Nevertheless, there has been a cultural censorship that has taken place about the role of fathers and stepfathers in our fairy stories. The Grimm Brothers, Jacob (1785–1863) and Wilhelm (1786–1859) made their first collections of German folk tales in 1812 and 1815 and in these tales there were cruel or vicious mothers or an evil father. However after the first publication of *Kinder- und Hausmarchen* (*Children and Household Tales*), the cruelty was softened and changed as these tales became popular and widely disseminated and wicked fathers became ineffective fathers and mothers became stepmothers. This softening of the tales was reinforced by Edgar Taylor, who in 1823 translated them into English as *German Popular* Tales.[8]

The reason for this cultural censorship by the Grimm Brothers of the fairy stories that originally contained unkind mothers and fathers rested upon their political and philosophical ambitions. At the beginning of the nineteenth century Germany was still a collection of warring states and the Grimm Brothers hoped that, by collecting up traditional folk tales, the German bourgeoisie would come to appreciate that there lay in the German psyche a language and a tradition that could bring them all together. As Neil McGregor (2014) in his recent book, *Germany: Memories of a Nation*, made clear, this was a sensitive moment in their history as they countered the threat of a Napoleonic invasion. But even if there was something noble about the Grimm Brothers' wish to unite their nation and bring about 'a German political and social renaissance . . . [in which] . . . the Germans had an identity that no foreign invader could eradicate,' McGregor does not mince his words in his critique of the way they went about it, namely by civilizing their German fairy stories. This meant that they eliminated aspects of the fairy story that did not accord with the ideal bourgeois family of the nineteenth century. And in so doing the Grimm's tales became little short of 'a particular kind of social engineering with strong political overtones.' One result has been that we have been left with tales that have obscured some of the more radical ideas that did not sit comfortably with the German ideals of the nineteenth-century family. This is pertinent to the discussion of the role of the father in their tales, because as McGregor points out the Brothers Grimm 'chose words, expressions and narrative forms of development that provided. . . [and] justified male domination within the bourgeois public sphere.'[9]

The idea that the language of the fairy story could be impregnable to a foreign invader adds an interesting dimension to the enduring description of the stepmother as wicked. It implies the idea that the stepmother must remain imprisoned in a language that sees her as an evil force in order to protect the mother's goodness. It also helps us to see why the father needed to remain untouchable. By eliminating aspects of the fairy story that did not accord with the ideal patriarchal family of the nineteenth century, the Grimms' tales became not only a form of social and political engineering but they served to reinforce the idea of 'the children against the evil witch, the wicked stepmother, pretending to be kind.' The Grimm stories became a way of soothing social anxiety because the story always ended with beliefs about 'the bourgeois mother, with comforting words.'[10] Above all they became documents of the patriarchal values of reason against the superstitious folly of folk wisdom embodied as 'old wives' tales.'

The social pressure to change the image of the mother and exonerate the father in our fairy stories was not unique to Germany but was the result of the new social and cultural values that were emerging across Europe following the Reformation and Counter Reformation, which had brought such threat of chaos and social disintegration. To take just one example, the 'most striking feature of married life in eighteenth century England was the theoretical, legal and practical subordination of wives to their husbands, epitomized by the concept of patriarchy.'[11] So it is not surprising to find that an unruly wife needed to be censored out of our fairy stories and this was done by replacing her with a stepmother, who was after all to be found in many bereaved families. In this way the mother remained a safe and inviolate figure.

Industrialization played another significant part in the change that was taking place in the eighteenth and nineteenth century, as people moved away from rural life into crowded cities. This was a time of disequilibrium; poverty, food riots, revolution simmered and threatened the state, whether in England or Europe. It is therefore not surprising that the pre-literate tales of peasant life that were full of violence and cruelty and subversion needed to be refashioned. Their original vitality needed to become quietened so that the tale could uphold the belief in the patriarchal strength of the father. So we see that a critical appreciation of fathers underwent a change in our fairy stories as patriarchal authority asserted its pre-eminence. It was unimaginable that fathers were ever intent upon undermining society, unlike women, and so there was no need to project criticism away from them onto a stepfather. Yet, in spite of this cultural predisposition something more silent and subtle happens to those few tales in which fathers behave badly; they are put behind the nursery door, as it were, so that we hardly notice them and they never become part of the popular canon of children's fairy stories.

To give an example of what I mean, there is one version of the Cinderella tale that is scarcely known and is certainly not part of the pantheon of children's fairy stories. It appears in the seventeenth-century collection of Charles Perrault (1624–1703) under the title 'Donkey-Skin,' and in the later nineteenth-century collection of the Grimm Brothers, known as 'Allerleirauh.' The villain of the tale is Cinderella's lustful father. Cinderella's mother dies, and on her deathbed she says to her husband he must only marry another woman who is as beautiful as she is. Cinderella grows up and her father finds that she is the only woman who is as beautiful as his wife, and so he pursues her. She runs away and disguises herself in a donkey-skin, or in a coat of a 'thousand furs' and is finally rescued by a young prince who can see beyond her disguise. The father fades out of the tale and we hear nothing more about him.[12]

It is a tale that has similarities to the story of Zezolla's murderous hatred, not least because both Zezolla's murderous hatred and Cinderella's lustful father lie buried or half forgotten under the encroaching censorship. The challenging element in 'Donkey-Skin' is that there is a recognition that incestuous desire can lie at the heart of family life, and one might add, children need to know that parents are vulnerable to such impulses. But once this recognition gets eased out, some of the wisdom of such a folk tale gets lost. It is also notable that in this tale of a father's incestuous desire for his daughter there is no wicked stepmother lurking in the shadows.

There have been several interpretations of the differences in the Cinderella tale, with some saying that the 'Donkey-Skin' version has a different origin and should not be seen as the same 'type.'[13] But whatever the truth of that belief might be, it is significant that the most popular version of Cinderella today pushes the father almost out of sight and he becomes a vague and vanishing figure in the background. This is the case in the Cinderella tales in both Charles Perrault's *Historie ou Contes du Temps Passé (ou Contes de Ma Mère L'Oye)* in the seventeenth century, and the Grimm Brothers' *Kinder- und Hausmarchen* in the nineteenth century. These tales no longer carry the energy and violence of the original tales but instead they bear the hallmarks of the social and family values of their transcribers, not least the idealization of the mother who is always suitably dead.[14] As Tatar (1987) pointed out, 'It is easy to see why fairy stories which evolved only late in their development into stories for children, favour the theme of maternal malice over the forbidden and forbidding theme of incest.'[15]

It is regrettable that some of the power of the fairy story to engage with emotional difficulties within the family gets lost when the father is banished. The wrestling with such uncomfortable ideas as paternal desire needs to be spoken about and it is remarkable to think that the fairy story did provide helpful ways of confronting such situations. It would not be an exaggeration to say that when they were refashioned for popular consumption and for children, we lost a part of our minds. 'Our ancestors created therapeutic spaces that were more capacious and more communally orientated than the office chair and couch used today. "Thousandfurs" [another name for 'Donkey-Skin'] reminds us of the power of storytelling to foster dialogue, to heal and to assure survival.'[16]

Once the wicked father is sidelined for social and cultural reasons to do with the increasing emphasis on the patriarchal family, then one of the things that seems to happen is that the wicked stepmother steps in as a welcomed replacement and distraction from a tale about a sexually powerful father.[17] This becomes clear when Perrault asserted that 'Donkey-Skin' was no more than an 'old wives' tale.' By that he meant that there was no need to point an admonishing finger at the conduct of fathers because 'Donkey-Skin' was a fantastic tale that sprang from women's gossip and tittle-tattle.[18] It is not hard to imagine that such an attitude was clearly more comfortable for men like Perrault and later the Grimm Brothers as they collected these legends.[19]

The implicit passivity of the father in 'Donkey-Skin' is to be found in another uncomfortable tale about a father's unnatural desire, namely in the tale of 'The Maiden without Hands.' In the complete Grimm collection of two hundred and ten fairy tales, the Grimm Brothers have transformed the ending of the tale. This is their version. A father agrees to be helped out of his poverty by the devil, whose bargain is that he has to hand over the first thing that he sees when he returns home. He does not expect that it will be his daughter, which it is, but he nevertheless obeys the devil and puts up no fight to save his daughter. Instead he pleads with her, 'if I do not cut off both your hands, the Devil will carry me away, and in my terror I have agreed to do it.' He ends with a heartfelt plea, 'Help me in my need, and forgive me the harm I do you,' as he cuts off her hands.[20] It is a cruel tale and it certainly does not show the father in an admirable light. Yet the puzzle is that we are being asked to feel sorry for him as he asks for forgiveness from his daughter.

Why should we feel sorry for him? It is only when we learn that the Grimm Brothers had censored an even more disquieting element in the original story that the puzzle is made clear. In the earlier tale it is the girl who cuts off her hands as the day of her incestuous wedding to her father dawns and in this way she extracts herself from her father's desires. However for the Grimm Brothers and their readers, to be told of a girl cutting off her hands, as a way of extracting herself from her father's incestuous intrusion, would have brought attention to the father's inappropriate desire. It was safer to distract the reader from the true meaning of the tale and to say it was the work of the devil and that the father was penitent in the end.[21]

One of the interesting features about this father's pact with the devil is that unlike the women in our fairy stories, he is not transformed into a devil or a wizard himself when he makes his pact, and in this way we are distracted from any fear of the father. This is in marked contrast to the way stepmothers and fairy godmothers are thought about. They are all part of a universal belief that they are witches or old crones in disguise, even when dressed up as the good fairy in Cinderella or the fairy godmother in Snow White. All old women are to be feared because they may contain supernatural powers and their benevolence could be transformed into violence, in a word or a wish or the wave of a wand as they revert to their powerful pagan origins.[22] Fathers do not contain such magical powers and are never transformed into wizards and devils. They can be possessed by the devil, or sell their soul to him, but these are visitations of temporary madness and they do not have the same transformational effect upon the male character. I think we can safely say that a father who makes a pact with the devil never becomes evil in himself thereafter. The reason for this is that the father is never believed to be hiding a supernatural power that may suddenly emerge.

It is this fundamental difference between the mother/stepmother and the father/stepfather that is most noticeable in our fairy stories. The women have supernatural powers, the men do not, and one consequence is that fathers and stepfathers tend to slide out of the tale and be forgotten. We never have the satisfaction of finding that they are thrown into a cauldron of boiling water or roasted alive for their evil desires, and the final outrage is that they never receive just retribution. One nice example is the way the erring father is dealt with in Perrault's version of 'Donkey-Skin,' in his *Tales of Mother Goose*. It is told in humorous rhyming couplets, so we are already being asked to consider the tale as an amusing trifle. And in the final four lines this attitude of levity is confirmed.

> This tale is hard to credit, to be sure
> But yet, as long as children dwell
> Upon this earth, with mum and gran as well,
> Its memory will stay secure.[23]

In other words the misdemeanours of the father are merely 'old wives' tales' that have been invented by women, who had nothing better to do than to spend their days in idle gossip creating untruthful stories about men.[24] In this way we turn our gaze away from the transgressive behaviour of fathers.

In the twentieth century Bettelheim (1976) did something even more telling to the idea of a threatening male figure, when he re-interpreted the tale of *Little Red Riding Hood*. The tale was an eighteenth-century French fairy story in which Little Red Riding Hood is told by her mother to go and visit her grandmother and take her milk and bread. She is followed through the woods by a wolf, who gets to the grandmother's house first and kills her, then dresses in her clothes and pretends he is the grandmother. Little Red Riding Hood not only eats some of her grandmother, offered to her by the wolf as meat, but the wolf then eats her up.[25] This cruel and violent tale, that would seem to be a frightening warning to young girls about the predatory nature of men, becomes something quite different in the hands of Bettelheim. If we are appalled by the tale then that is because we have 'not achieved a satisfactory integration of the two worlds of reality and imagination,' he states. If we had achieved 'satisfactory integration' then we should not be – tempted? – to read the story as though it was about a male character, the wolf. We should understand that he is no more than 'the kindly grandmother [who] undergoes a sudden replacement.' A sheep in wolves' clothing? And in this way, wolves or men, fathers or stepfathers are not to be imagined as a threat, or a disturbing figure who seduces and devours; they are only women in wolves' clothing, and as an addendum, it is all in the child's mind anyway.[26] It is hard not to feel that Bettelheim's soothing understanding of *Little Red Riding Hood* is a travesty of the truth that the tale was trying to tell.

A more charitable view might be to say that Bettelheim was following in the footsteps of Freud, and wanting to prove the truth of Freud's understanding of the developing infant mind by showing how the fairy story depicted the child's unconscious anxieties. Bettelheim wished to do this by demonstrating that the enduring power of our fairy stories was that they described the child's mind as it struggled with its Oedipal desires. But today this Freudian model is seen as too narrow, and some of the most far reaching criticisms of Freud have come from those who have brought to our attention that he ignored the impact of parental fantasies, wishes and desires upon the child.[27] He ignored the wisdom of the fairy stories that are concerned with the destructive impact that adults can have upon children.

What could be said about Freud was that he wove his own fairy stories, especially when, like the Grimm Brothers, he was told some uncomfortable tales about fathers. It is well known that Freud changed his belief that his hysterical female patients were suffering from the sexual abuse of their father to a later belief that many of his hysterical women patients were under the spell of a sexual fantasy or wish. Yet there are parallels in the shifting emphasis in Freud's understanding of paternal sexual abuse and the cultural censorship that has taken place in our fairy stories. Both Freud and the Grimm Brothers have had difficulty in facing the extent of sexual abuse of children at the hands of fathers/stepfathers.

It is not my intention to enter into the discussion that was occasioned by Masson's (1985) *The Assault on the Truth* when he accused Freud of turning away from the extent of child abuse that was taking place in nineteenth-century Vienna.[28] Freud never denied that sexual abuse could occur, but what he did deny was that it was always the reason for the hysterical phenomenon that he observed in his female patients; he was to suggest that the hysterical symptom could be the result of repressed sexual fantasies in the mind of the patient. However, once Freud does distinguish between these two possible causes for hysterical phenomenon, there follows an uneasy alliance between fantasy and reality, or as Freud put it, 'The outcome is the same, and up to the present we have not succeeded in pointing to any difference in the consequences, whether phantasy or reality has had the greater share in these events in childhood.'[29]

This uneasy alliance is to be seen in one of Freud's early case histories, that not only reads like a fairy story but has similarities to the toning down of the fairy stories about father/daughter incest that have been considered above. Katharina appears in Freud's and Breuer's *Studies in Hysteria*, and from the first Freud draws the reader into an enchanting world, as he was to admit:

> It still strikes me as strange that the case histories I write should read like short stories and that, as one might say, they lack the serious stamp of science. I must console myself with the reflection that the nature of the subject is evidently responsible for this, rather than any preference of my own.[30]

He begins this particular clinical case in the following way, 'In the summer vacation of the year 189– I made an excursion into the Hohe Tauern so that for a while I might forget medicine and more particularly neuroses.' And he goes on to say as he walked up the mountain, 'I turned aside from the main road to climb a mountain which lay some way apart.' We are surely near the magical forest where all sorts of extraordinary events may occur, and it is indeed a transforming tale. Some time after his arrival Freud is sitting on the terrace of this inn 'lost in thought' after his strenuous climb, and while he is admiring the view, the young daughter of his landlady asks him if she could talk to him. She says she is suffering from 'nerves.' In the course of their conversation Freud helped her to recognize that her 'nerves' were her way of denying the trauma of having been sexually abused by her uncle. Once she was helped by Freud's questions to recognize that this was true but had been repressed, 'She was like someone transformed. The sulky, unhappy face had grown lively, her eyes were bright, she was lightened and exalted.' And that brief conversation brought the 'therapy' to a close.[31]

I do not doubt that Freud helped her and that furthermore he was fearless in getting her to see that she had been sexually abused, which was an unacceptable idea in the late nineteenth century in Vienna. But the point I want to make is that Freud himself later reveals that the uncle was in fact her father and it is this point that brings me back to the fairy story.[32] Intellectually we might be sympathetic to Freud's argument that he changed the father to the uncle for reasons of discretion, but I want to suggest that behind this discretion lies another social and cultural pressure, to which Freud bowed: the wish to exculpate the father.

So where does this lead us in trying to understand why fathers and stepfathers fare better in our fairy stories? And how can we explain the fact that fathers behaving badly appear much less frequently than mothers or stepmothers? Has it always been more expedient to warn the young that they may have a more difficult time with matriarchal women? Or has there been a more general reluctance even within the oral narrative of our legends and fairy stories to face predatory and destructive males?

Warner (1995) has suggested that many of our early oral tales could be read as 'old wives' tales' told by women as a self-help manual for young girls on how to manage powerful and dominating women or mothers-in-law. In other words there were robust tales that did not flinch from the fact that women could be powerful and cruel and were capable of being as misogynistic as any man. We also have a few robust tales about fathers and their desire for their beautiful daughters if there is no mother around. But once the male transcribers, such as the Grimm Brothers, begin to collect our fairy stories, and when later they fall under the hands of male interpreters, such as Bettelheim, these tales of male transgression are pushed out of popular sight. They hardly exist, and if they do they are either 'old wives' tales' or all in the mind of the child anyway.

One reason for the sidelining of fairy tales about father/daughter incest is that there has been a cultural wish to deny the place that father/daughter incest has had in the history of the family. It has always been seen as more heinous and more ubiquitous than maternal incest yet there has been a universal wish to deny this fact.[33] One way out of this conundrum has been to blame someone else. In Freud's case of Katharina the public blame first fell upon her uncle, not her father. It was only thirty years later and after the First World War that Freud believed that it would not be indiscreet to publish the true fact that Katherina had been abused by her father. By then the world had been turned upside down and the reality of the internal world of the imagination, so revered by the Romantic poets and by the early psychoanalysts, was thrown into disarray. The ineluctable impressions of the external world on those who survived the war were beginning to demand a different way of thinking about the complex relationship between social events, cultural values and the way we see the world.[34]

One result of the failure to give equal space to male transgression in our fairy stories has been that fathers and stepfathers in the real world today do not carry the same negative legacy as stepmothers; they are not burdened with the archetypal image of being potentially wicked and there is the temptation to believe that if they have any faults, it is merely a case of dereliction, as was the case with Cinderella's father. But a troubling cultural problem remains. The present day stepmother is still unfairly burdened with a legacy from our oral tradition of storytelling; whereas the father/stepfather has escaped from this imaginative legacy, through the censorship of transcribers and interpreters, but this has left a vacuum.

In banishing the father from the popular canon of our fairy stories, we are depriving ourselves of a more considered appreciation of the truth of such a tale as 'Donkey-Skin.' Children need to be made aware that fathers and stepfathers can sometimes be a threat and that incestuous desire does not just reside in the harmless Oedipal fantasies that the child projects onto the parents. The more robust tales that were an attempt to explain adult desires and adult cruelty need to be brought back into the canon of children's fairy stories and read to them, not least because they provide children with some imaginative support for the idea that there are means of escaping unwanted intrusion. Not, I have to add, by cutting off your hands, as in 'The Maiden without Hands,' nor by pretending that the unwanted intrusion did not occur, but by being made aware that male desire can get out of control.

One interesting consequence of softening the behaviour of the father is that in many of our fairy stories he is a very ineffective father. In Cinderella he is sent off on long journeys and when he returns home he does not notice that his wife is mistreating his daughter, and we are left with the impression that he would not have dared to stand up to his wife in any case. It is as though, for the collectors of these tales, there can only be a wimpish good father who is ineffective in protecting his daughter because he is always absenting himself; or there is a predatory father who is far too present and he needs to be sidelined.

This leads me to add a postscript to the vacuum that was left when the father was censored out of our fairy tales. It is tempting to wonder whether the censorship of our fairy stories about sexually predatory fathers or stepfathers is at last being confronted and our society is beginning to recognize that child abuse happens, and it is not just in the mind of the child.[35] The history of the way the child has been thought about, whether East or West, reveals over and over again a failure to imagine that a child has a mind that is distinguishable from the mind of an adult. Part of Freud's genius was to begin to give us a template in order to imagine this difference. But this knowledge, that the child has a mind that is different from that of an adult, and that a child does not have the same sexual desires as an adult, is constantly confounded, as our daily reports about child sexual abuse show us.

This takes me back to the fairy story. The damage that was done to the fairy story when it was turned into a tale for children meant that children were no longer exposed to the stories of ill-considered adult passions. By that I mean, what was imposed on them was the false belief that these fairy stories were tales about their own desires and wishes. In so doing, what got lost was the knowledge that many of these tales were an attempt to explain that adult desires and adult cruelty were a fact of life. Once these tales were retold as children's fairy stories, it was only a short step to have children believe that if they feared parental sexual desire, it was all in their mind, and had nothing to do with a real apprehension of the threat of inappropriate adult behaviour. Before the printing press, children who listened to the early oral tales about incest, cruelty and death were much better informed about the behaviour of adults. We need to find a way of telling them again that fathers and stepfathers, as well as mothers and stepmothers, can behave badly.

Notes

1 Tatar (1987): There are '2 or 3 wicked fathers to be found in the Grimm Fairy Stories and 13 wicked stepmothers' (p. 308 n. 17).
2 Bettelheim (1976) p. 114.
3 Zipes (1979) p. 195.
4 Coles (2015).
5 Stone (1990) p. 48.
6 Weber (1981) cites the case of an eighteenth-century father who sired thirty-two children with three mothers, two of whom treated their stepchildren with great cruelty (p. 93). Also Klapsich-Zuber (1987), in Tuscany in the fifteenth century, 'from 75 to 100 percent of all men [who were widowers] up to the age of 60 years took another wife' (p. 120). Again, Weber (1981) in France, 'during the seventeenth and eighteenth centuries between 20% and 80% of widowers remarried within the year of their spouse's death' (p. 112).
7 Zipes (2002), Bettelheim (1976).
8 Zipes (2002): 'Taylor's successful Anglicization and infantilization of the tales set a "mode" for the literary fairy in England in the nineteenth century' (p. 112). Also Warner (1995) who shows the way the Grimm Brothers tinkered, evaded and suppressed those bits that caused them anxiety (p. 347).
9 McGregor (2014) pp. 117–123.
10 McGregor (2014) p. 117.
11 Stone (1990): '[t]he unity of Christendom . . . had been irreparably shattered by the Reformation . . . the pieces were never put together again.' With the result that '[t]he authoritarian family and the authoritarian nation state were the solutions to an intolerable sense of anxiety, and a deep yearning for order' (pp. 145–146).

12 Grimm (1972) p. 283.
13 See Ralston (1982) on types of folktale (pp. 30–56).
14 See Tatar (1987) and Zipes (1979).
15 Tatar (1987) p. 155.
16 Tatar (1987) p. 241.
17 'What appears natural in the Grimm's tales was not natural in the oral folk tradition' (Zipes 2002 p. 57).
18 'old wives' tales poised between wisdom and folly' (Warner 1995 p. 14).
19 See Warner (1995), in particular the influence of Colbert on Perrault in which 'tale-telling' was 'the domain of midwives, layers-out and witches' (p. 36). Also Zipes (2002) on the Grimm Brothers: 'their ethics [in the tales] assumed the form of self-validation of patriarchy in the family and male domination in the public realm' (p. 13).
20 Grimm (2002) p. 134.
21 It was Warner (1995) who suggested the tale was about a 'father's unlawful love' for his daughter with the savaging 'accent on the role of hands in sexuality' (p. 348).
22 Zipes (2012): 'The "great accomplishment" of Christianity was its transformation of goddesses, sorceresses and fairies into demonic and malevolent figures' (p. 77). Also Warner (1995), 'The word "fairy" . . . indicates a meaning of the wonder or fairy tales . . . which refers to a goddess of destiny' (pp. 14–15).
23 Perrault (2009) p. 77.
24 Warner (1995) gives the following account of the history of gossip: 'Both the linguistic link between godmothers and old gossips, and the social link between ageing women and secret, wicked powers, are crucial in the world of the fairy tale; wresting control of that evil tongue occupied the energies of many of the pioneers of the nursery tales' (p. 48).
25 Darnton (1984) pp. 9–10.
26 Bettelheim (1976) p. 66.
27 Laplanche and Pontalis (1964).
28 Masson (1984).
29 Freud (1916–1917) p. 370.
30 Freud and Breuer (1895) p. 160.
31 Freud and Breuer (1893–1895) pp. 125–131.
32 See footnote added in 1924 p. 134.
33 There is an extensive literature on incest, but to take three examples, de Mause (1991) Finkelhor (1983) and Matsakis (1991) all suggest that incest perpetrated by fathers, uncles and stepfathers is more frequent.
34 For example, Bion (1984), Bowlby (1969, 1973) and Solms (2002).
35 *The Guardian*, 19 January 2016. A Junior Shadow Minister suggested that there should be compulsory lessons for all children in primary schools that 'what is in their pants is private.' It is estimated that 500,000 children are being abused, emotionally, physically and sexually.

References

Bettelheim, B. (1976) *The Uses of Enchantment: The Meaning and Importance of Fairy Tales*. Harmondsworth: Penguin Books Ltd.
Bion, W.R. (1984) *Second Thoughts*. London: Karnac Books.
Bowlby, J. (1969, 1973) *Attachment*. Vol. I and II. London: Hogarth Press.
Coles, P. (2015) *The Shadow of the Second Mother: Nurses and Nannies in Theories of Infant Development*. London/New York: Routledge.
Darnton, R. (1984) *The Great Cat Massacre: And Other Episodes in French Cultural History*. New York: Basic Books.

De Mause, L. (1991) The Universality of Incest. *Journal of Psychohistory.* 19. 2: 1–34.

Finklehor, D. (1983) *The Dark Side of the Family: Current Family Violence Research.* Newbury Park: Sage Publications.

Freud, S. and Breuer, J. (1895) Studies in Hysteria. In *The Standard Edition of the Complete Psychological Works of Sigmund Freud. Vol. 2.* London: Hogarth Press.

Freud, S. (1916–1917) Introductory Lectures on Psychoanalysis. In *The Standard Edition of the Complete Psychological Works of Sigmund Freud. Vol. 15–16.* London: Hogarth Press.

Grimm, J and W. (2002) *Complete Fairy Tales.* London/New York: Routledge.

Klapisch-Zuber, C. (1985) *Women, Family and Ritual in Renaissance Italy.* Chicago/London: Chicago University Press.

Lang, A. (2006 [1903]) *Crimson Fairy Book.* Dover: Children's Classics.

Laplanche, J. and Pontalis, J.B. (1964) Fantasy and the origins of sexuality. *International Journal of Psychoanalysis.* 49: 1–18.

MacGregor, N. (2014) *Germany: Memories of a Nation.* Allen Lane: Penguin Books.

Masson, J.M. (1984) *The Assault on the Truth: Freud's Suppression of the Seduction Theory.* New York: Farrar, Straus & Giroux.

Matsakis, A. (1991) *When the Bough Breaks.* Oakland, CA: New Harbinger Publications.

Perrault, C. (2009 [1697]) *The Complete Fairy Tales.* Trans C. Betts. Oxford/New York: Oxford University Press.

Ralston, W.R.S. (1982) Cinderella. In A. Dundes Ed. *Cinderella: A Casebook.* London/Wisconsin: University of Wisconsin Press.

Solms, M. and Turnbull, O. (2002) *The Brain and the Inner World.* New York: Other Press.

Stone, L. (1990) *The Family, Sex and Marriage in England 1500–1800.* London: Penguin Books.

Tatar, M. (1987) *The Hard Facts of the Grimms' Fairy Tales* (2nd edition). Princeton/Woodstock: Princeton University Press.

Warner, M. (1995) *From the Beast to the Blonde. On Fairy Tales and Their Tellers.* London: Vintage Books.

Weber, E. (1981) Fairies and Hard Facts: The Reality of Folk Tales. *Journal of the History of Ideas.* 42: 93–113.

Zipes, J. (1979) *Breaking the Magic Spell: Radical Theories of Folk and Fairy Tales.* Kentucky: University Press of Kentucky.

Zipes, J. (2002) *The Brothers Grimm: From Enchanted Forests to the Modern World.* New York/Basingstoke: Palgrave Macmillan.

Zipes, J. (2012) *The Irresistible Fairy Tale: The Cultural and Social History of a Genre.* Princeton/Woodstock: Princeton University Press.

Chapter 3

The strangely shaped footprint of women

In order to understand more fully the prejudice we have against the stepmother and the more lenient view we have towards fathers and stepfathers, I need to step back into the past and be guided by those who have been interested in early civilization and the role that women have played through the millennia. The question I shall be addressing in this chapter is, do we hate the stepmother because she is not the real mother, or, do we catch a glimpse of something more frightening when the stepmother appears? Is the stepmother wrapped in the cloak of an ancient civilization? Does she still arouse the suspicion that she needs placating lest she wreaks her revenge? This idea that the fear of stepmother has links with the world of pagan goddesses is not as far-fetched as it sounds. Hera, the wife of Zeus, has been described from Homer onwards as the earliest depiction of an evil stepmother and so the mythological associations between Hera and the stepmother have an ancient history.

However before we can understand how Hera acquired her description as an evil stepmother, we need to understand the ancient civilization from which Hera sprang and how she became transformed from a pagan goddess of fertility into the jealous and destructive wife of Zeus when they married. In tracing her history we can begin to feel some sympathy for her and perhaps see some reason for her jealous behaviour towards her 'stepson' Herakles. Hera came to be seen as an evil stepmother because she was angry with Zeus' treatment of her. He demeaned and humiliated her and yet her anger was attributed to be a character fault, not a result of her experience at the hands of her husband. When their marriage took place Zeus was believed to be the supreme god who ruled over everyone and needed to be obeyed, and from the moment of his ascendancy a significant change in the relationship between men and women in Western culture took place. Hera lost her status as a goddess of fertility and in Homeric legend she came to be seen as the first evil stepmother. This has had a lasting and damaging impact upon our beliefs about stepmothers, and we have forgotten that some of the language we use to describe the stepmother has been fashioned in the image of Hera.

I think that we can all have an intuitive sense that Zeus' domination of Hera gives her sufficient reason to be angry, but there has been a tendency to turn a blind eye to the thought that the domination by men makes women resentful.

Instead women's anger has been attributed to certain types of women such as jealous goddesses and stepmothers. The beauty of this argument is that we can then believe that women after all can be trusted; it is only the stepmother who is the suspicious and untrustworthy character. In other words the stepmother has projected onto her the mistrustful feelings men can have about women. But there is another subtle twist to this belief; it is not only men who project their fear of the anger of women onto the stepmother, but women also project their fear of powerful women onto the stepmother. In such cases the stepmother can become the symbolic representation of the women's angry feelings that they have not dared to express. On this account, the stepmother is freighted with her mythological representations. She carries the split-off fear that men have harboured about women and at the same time she embodies women's fear of their own evil thoughts and destructive wishes. This latter idea will become clear as we consider Hera's treatment of her stepson Herakles.

Before Zeus became the god of Hellenic culture, Hera was a pagan goddess of fertility in the pre-Hellenic world surrounding the Mediterranean basin, with temples on Samos and Athos, and she had a revered cult in Crete. What led me back to Hera and her representation as the archetypal image of the stepmother was reading the opening words of D.A. Mackenzie's (1917) *Crete and Pre-Hellenic Myths and Legends*: 'In relating how Crete has risen into prominence as the seat of a great and ancient civilization, one is reminded of the fairy story of Cinderella.'[1] These words stimulated me to think further about Cinderella and her stepmother and Hera. I discovered that Mackenzie was not interested in the Cinderella fairy story and her troubles with her stepmother; he was using the metaphor of her lost slipper to describe Schliemann's belief that there was a pre-Hellenic civilization lying hidden on this island. Nonetheless I wondered whether this pre-Hellenic society may have more associations to Cinderella than the lost slipper, namely could some of our beliefs about the stepmother have links with pagan beliefs about such a goddess as Hera? Are we still haunted by a belief that the stepmother is a witch-like figure with deadly intentions, imprisoned in 'her ancient savage character'?[2] Or, put another way, are the footprints of these beliefs about the matriarchal goddesses still to be found in the images we hold about the stepmother?

The pre-Hellenic civilization of Crete was thriving from 10000 BC until 1000 BC, and Hera was one of the most important goddesses revered for her wisdom and creativity as well as representing the three stages of a woman's life, her virginity, her fertility and her old age. The beliefs in Hera grew out of an even earlier and primordial belief that our destiny was held in the hands of the Three Fates or Moirae, one who spun the thread of our destiny, one who determined the life we would lead and one who cut the thread of life. And here, perhaps as in no other myth, we can see how deeply entrenched was the belief that women determined not only our life but our fate.[3] However, though the Three Fates and later the early matriarchal goddesses were believed to bring light and life to mankind, they also needed propitiating because their varying moods could bring floods or famine. 'Now she was the earth serpent ... and ... the raven of death; she might also appear as the mountain hag followed by savage beasts, or as a composite monster in a gloomy cave.'[4]

It has been generally accepted that the beliefs that sustained the pre-Hellenic period were gradually eclipsed when the Hellenes, the Northern barbarians, invaded Greece and brought with them a new set of beliefs. These invaders were said to be 'Sky-God-worshiping . . . [and] brought new patriarchal beliefs and laws and pushed out the beliefs of the Earth-Goddess-worshiping, matrilineal pre-Hellenic inhabitants.'[5] The Olympian gods now determined man's fate and Zeus became all powerful. He married Hera and there the trouble started. Hera no longer had her own temples of worship and was never consulted for her wisdom; instead she found herself kept in her place under Zeus.

I do not want to deride the importance of this cultural change. Our Western civilization has been based upon the belief in the superiority of Greek rational thought that in turn grew out of Hellenic beliefs in the superiority of the gods over the matriarchal goddesses. We still hold that Socratic reasoning, as Plato argued, would bring about a more measured life and this became the foundation stone of the Enlightenment belief that if we could measure and collect and publish all our knowledge then 'this would lead to the improvement of humanity.'[6] These ideas have played an essential part in Western democracy and are both much needed and valued; but my argument is that there has been a dark thread that has continually woven its way into this picture and subverted the pattern. What we find is that in spite of believing that we are no longer threatened by superstition and the need to make sacrifices and placatory offerings to savage goddesses, when it comes to thinking about women, and stepmothers in particular, they still arouse deep and irrational fears. There are some enduring myths about women that have left their footprint upon our imagination, forcing us to recognize that reason has not overthrown these superstitions. We may think that female goddesses have been superseded by the gods with their patriarchal laws of reason but some of their ghostly traces remain.

Hera's character underwent a radical change when she joined the Greek pantheon and was married to Zeus, and along with her change of character we catch a glimpse of what gradually became the changing status of women in Western culture. Zeus appropriated her and dominated her and their marriage was a furious tempest of disagreement.[7] On Homeric accounts the Trojan War was acerbated by the disharmony that existed between them and Hera came off the worst.[8] She became discredited and gained a bad reputation and as one historian sympathetically put it, 'Hera seems to suffer something of loss of status in Homer and becomes almost a comic figure.'[9] Finally we find her in our myths as a jealous and envious woman whose most particular crime was to try and destroy her stepson, Herakles, and so she became the archetypal evil stepmother.

In the myth of Hera as 'stepmother,' Zeus had an affair with Alcmene, said to be a human, and with whom he had a son, Herakles. Hera was furious with Zeus for his adultery and she hated her 'stepson' for he reminded her of Zeus' betrayal.[10] She did all she could to destroy Herakles. It is not necessary to go into the legendary lengths to which she went in her attempt to get rid of him; suffice it to say, her destructive deeds served to highlight Herakles' strength and he became one of the great heroes in the Greek pantheon. Meanwhile Hera became the 'model of jealousy and strife,' and what gets forgotten is that she was angry at Zeus' betrayal.[11] This image of Hera as the wicked destructive 'stepmother,' who tries her best to get rid of her 'stepson' Herakles, still affects our imagination when we think about the stepmother, and this fear is augmented by a question that has seldom been asked: why would a woman, like Hera, who was revered as a goddess of fertility and wisdom, suddenly become this ferocious jealous and destructive woman towards Herakles?

It seems clear from several scholars of early Greek civilization that the discoveries made by Schliemann and Evans at the end of the nineteenth century and early twentieth century found a very different and more peaceful world from the one described by Homer, and later writers such as Hesiod.[12] Homer's legends of the Greek heroes have much in common with the Grimm Brothers. They are all essentially masculine tales of the hero or the heroine whose lives were pitted against a malign figure who might be a wicked witch or a destructive stepmother. The Homeric legends or the Grimms' tales brought a masculine slant to the way women were thought about and described, and men have had a much easier time in their legends. What gets left out is that Hera and her subsequent mythological incarnations may have had good reason to rail against masculine rule and injustice.

Men have resisted this knowledge and instead they became anxious about women who were believed to be concealing all sorts of unknown threats to masculine pride. For instance, Freud wrote that trying to understand the psyche of women was like coming across an ancient civilization that was 'grey with age, and shadowy and almost impossible to revivify.'[13] What may have obscured Freud's difficulty in understanding the female psyche was his indebtedness to Greek mythology. His favourite Greek figurine who sat on his desk was Athena. She was a goddess who was not born of a woman but had sprung out of Zeus' head because Zeus had swallowed Metis, Athena's mother. Was Athena such an important goddess for Freud because she had never been born of woman? What we do know, as Jacobs (2017) pertinently pointed out,

> the denial of Athena's mother has resulted in the prevention of the myth effectively being used in psychoanalytic theory as a model or structure that can account for fantasies and unconscious processes that are not reducible to the Oedipus/patriarchal structure.[14]

I want to use Freud as an example of the anxiety many men have faced when trying to fit women into a masculine way of thinking. Freud's belief that encountering the psyche of women was like coming across an ancient civilization that was 'grey with age, and shadowy and almost impossible to revivify' may have concealed his intuitive knowledge that women could not be suborned in the way

Zeus had attempted with Metis or with Hera. Zeus may have been an early hero of Hellenic thought and this had helped to give rise to a belief in the power of masculine reason, but the repression of women, their creativity and their anger has augmented their threat.

One of the clearest examples of the anxiety about women and their desires is to be found in the Old Testament in the mysterious legend of King Solomon and the Queen of Sheba. Who was this mythical woman, with her spices and herbs, why did she come visiting Solomon, and what was her desire? The link to the mythological status of the stepmother as evil may at this stage seem tenuous, but in following some of the ways man has tried to answer the question, posed by the legend of the Queen of Sheba, we may be able to see more clearly that the stepmother has also become a depository for men and women's deepest fears about the power of the sexuality of women. The ancient and imponderable question about women's desire has been asked, in many different ways, and in many different languages, once man believed that he had begun to bring order to the more savage beliefs of the Earth Mother. But the answer has always ended up with a myth or legend that a woman's wish is to sexually devour the man, whether the tale comes from the East or the West. To return to the legend of King Solomon and the Queen of Sheba, it has been said to be a tale that attempts to make a coherent narrative out of Arab paganism and Judaic and Christian beliefs.[15] But what keeps breaking out of this tale and disrupting the wished for order is the question of the Queen of Sheba's desires; 'she is marked by heterodoxy, a marginal woman, like the Sybils, who never quite belongs in the fold, yet exercises power.'[16] It needs to be said that there are no historical records of the existence of the Queen of Sheba, though there are records of a third-century Arab queen called Bilqis, whereas King Solomon is known to have existed around 900 BC.[17] These facts have not deterred Christians and Muslims and Jews from claiming that it is a tale that exemplifies the conversion from paganism to true faith, or ordered reason over the unruly worshipping of elemental forces.

In the meeting between Sheba and Solomon, 'she came to prove him with a hard question' and what happened when they met was that 'she communed with him of all that was in her heart/ And Solomon told her all her questions and there was not *any* thing hid from the king, which he told her not.' The story goes on to say that she was deeply impressed by his wisdom and faith and became converted from her pagan beliefs, 'And King Solomon gave unto the Queen of Sheba all her desire' and she returned home.[18] Much of course hangs upon what was the queen's desire that Solomon satisfied; was it just her curiosity or was there something more to her desire? And it is around this question that the many subsequent tales about her have been spread.

For instance, in the Qu'ran, seven hundred years after the biblical account, the Queen of Sheba has a very different experience when she meets Solomon. She lifts her skirts as she walks across Solomon's courtyard, believing that it is covered in water, not in glass, and in exposing her legs, that were said to be hairy, her pagan origins are revealed. Her legs were never to be forgotten as their symbolic meaning become elaborated in tales that spread into Christianized Europe in the Middle Ages. Warner richly illustrates the transformation of Sheba from an exotic pagan queen who brought spices to Solomon to a she-devil with a cloven hoof who in some quarters became known as the whore of Babylon for her 'gifts included something more than material goods, and she is represented expressing desire: her body moves, her flesh breathes in a way that Solomon's does not.'[19]

It may seem that I have strayed a long way from Hera and her associations with the evil stepmother, but the myth of the Queen of Sheba and the myth surrounding Hera both describe the way paganism gave way to more orthodox beliefs about women, and it is here that we may need to look in order to deepen our understanding of the unconscious prejudice we have against the stepmother. Warner suggests the question that confronts those who want to bring these legends into a more reasoned narrative is how to bring these matriarchal goddesses into the fold; how could they be made to lie down and pose no threat? One way, in the myth of Hera, is to rob her of her protest at the way Zeus treated her, and to see her as a jealous and destructive stepmother who is angry that Zeus has produced a child that is not hers. The other way is to characterize women as a latter day Queen of Sheba, a she-devil with hairy legs and a cloven hoof who wants to seduce men. Once these matriarchal beliefs gave way to patriarchal order, there was a troublesome anxiety about the nature of women and mothers in particular. Who were they and what did they want? One way out of that difficulty was to turn mothers into idealized figures, as in the spread of the Christian belief in the Virgin Mary who became this emblematic icon. Then difficult or protesting women could be seen as treacherous stepmothers like Hera or lascivious whores as with the Queen of Sheba, and in many cases the stepmother was believed to have the characteristics of both.

This characteristic of troublesome woman has remained a dark thread of unconscious anxiety about what they desire and has continued to be asked throughout the centuries even up to the present day. There is one delightfully robust and ironic riposte to the question of women's desire, in Chaucer's (1343–1400) *The Canterbury Tales*, that serves to highlight man's anxiety while doing nothing to answer the question. It is a tale set at the time of King Arthur and told by the Wife of Bath. It concerns a knight who rapes a young girl, and this was of course against the chivalric order of courtly love and so the knight was to lose his head.[20] However the knight's life was to be spared if he could answer the question, 'What is the thing that women most desire?' The successful answer that spared the knight's life was that, 'A woman wants the self-same sovereignty over her husband as her lover and master him.'[21] This answer, as Coghill (1962) points out in his introduction to *The Canterbury Tales*, upset the cultural belief of the time that 'It was for the husband to command and the wife to obey.'[22] The twist to the tale is that the knight is then forced into marrying the old woman who gave him the true answer. Chaucer seems to be saying that knowing that a woman wanted to be equal to her husband opened up a door that was better left shut.[23]

But there is more to this tale and women's desire that brings us back to the stepmother. It is not clear in Chaucer's tale whether the knight is Lancelot, but assuming that it is, then we know from Mallory's *Morte D'Arthur* that at the end of Arthur's life he has to confront the question of Queen Guinevere's adultery with Lancelot, to which he had all his life turned a blind eye.[24] When he finally goes to France to confront Lancelot with this truth, he learns that his illegitimate son, Mordred, has annexed his kingdom in England, and has imprisoned Guinevere. He returns to England to fight Mordred and he knows that it will end in the death of both of them. At that moment he cries out, 'Ah! Fortune, contrary and changeable ... You used to be my mother now you have become my stepmother, and to make me die of grief you brought Death with you.'[25]

The transformation of fortune from having been a good mother into a stepmother, who is a messenger of death, is not unfamiliar in our fairy stories but what is never made explicit in them is that the stepmother has associations with sexuality and adultery. It was only when Arthur had to face Guinevere's adultery that he was goaded into battle, and the good mother, Fortune, enters as the stepmother in a new habit, a woman with adulterous and sexually voracious wishes.[26]

The implications for the image of the stepmother take on a new and ambiguous turn, as she becomes associated with adultery. The concept of adultery has a complicated history when it comes to women's behaviour, and a woman's adultery has always been seen as more reprehensible than that of a man, not least because if men could not keep their wives under sexual control they could never be sure of their children's paternity. This was extremely important when inheritance determined the division of wealth and privilege for those who either possessed it or aspired to possess it.[27]

I now want to turn to the real world and the way adultery has been thought about from the early Middle Ages until the Divorce Law of 1857, not least because the place of the stepmother changes. Until the nineteenth century the stepmother had usually replaced the dead mother. Now with the fall in maternal mortality, in the nineteenth century, the stepmother entered the family not because the mother had died, but more often because she was chosen as more attractive than the woman she replaced. And along with this subtle shift from being associated with death, she now becomes associated with adultery and sexuality.

It has never been of great social, cultural or legal consequence if a man committed adultery, even though marriage, whether under Protestant or Catholic laws, was always believed to be 'until death do us part.' But a fearsome fate has been visited upon women's infidelity throughout recorded history, reflecting man's intuitive anxiety that women are not to be trusted and a belief that their adulterous behaviour could lead to the destruction of society. In the late eighteenth century the Bishop of Rochester claimed that women's adultery 'sapped the morality and manners of the people ... [and] ... and our country ... if once it is sunk in dissoluteness and abandoned immorality, will soon fall prey to corruption and slavery.'[28]

Medieval canon law absolutely forbade divorce, though there were ways of getting out of an unhappy marriage if one was rich. Until the Divorce Law of 1857, marital separation was only legally possible if the wife had committed adultery, but women could not divorce if their husbands were unfaithful. They had to put up with their husband's affairs. If women protested against their powerlessness and the social and legal inequality they lived under, they were shunned by their society, just as whistleblowers today are being cast into prison or having to live in exile.

'My husband can cheat me because I am his wife' wrote Caroline Norton in 1853, reflecting on the injustice of the case brought against her by her husband George Norton.[29] This was a particularly notorious case that in the end did help to bring about the Divorce Law of 1857, but not before the untold suffering of Caroline Norton and her three sons. This case was brought by George Norton against Lord Melbourne whom he said was in 'criminal conversation' with his wife Caroline Norton. The euphemism, 'criminal conversation,' seemed to have been a particularly complicated male idea that was at its height in the late eighteenth and nineteenth century. An aggrieved husband might bring a case against a man whom he suspected of having an adulterous relationship with his wife. This was the 'criminal conversation.' In such a case the wife had no right of reply, and the husband usually had to rely upon servants to verify his suspicion. The Norton v Melbourne case in 1836 brought London to a standstill.[30] Had Lord Melbourne and Caroline Norton had a 'criminal conversation'? The trial lasted all one hot summer's day in a room that had little air and was packed with the curious public, and the witnesses for the prosecution were a variety of past and unreliable servants who had worked for the Norton family. Finally at 11.30 pm the jury were asked to give their judgment and they returned within ten minutes with their verdict. 'My Lord, we are agreed. It is my duty to say that we have agreed to a verdict for the defendant.'[31]

It might have been hoped that Caroline Norton would now be allowed to divorce her husband George Norton. What she discovered was that the only way she could divorce him was to prove his adultery, and up until that moment she had no justification for that. What she also discovered was that if she lived apart from him he had the power over his children, and in this case he ruled that she should not see them again. She had three sons who were born in 1829, 1831 and 1833, and though of course she had nurses and nannies to look after her children, she was nevertheless a devoted mother. Norton sent them out of London, as far away as possible from his wife, to the unloving care of Norton's childless sister in Scotland. Caroline was naturally devastated, and suffered unimaginable grief when in 1842 her youngest son died after falling from his pony, without her being at his bedside, even though his last words were to call for her. Caroline did get to see her two surviving sons from time to time following her son Charles' death, but by that time they were quite psychologically damaged children and they never thrived.

Caroline was a gifted writer and a fearsome defender of what she considered her rights as a mother, and for twenty years she fought for a change in the law so that divorced women were no longer their husband's possession and they had legal rights to their own money and to their earnings and to their children. This eventually became part of the 1857 Divorce Law. Now women could be awarded custody of their children and if a wife was brought to trial for adultery she had the right to reply and perhaps most importantly of all divorces were now to be settled in civil courts and were no longer under the power of ecclesiastical courts or Parliament.[32]

The shift in the divorce law that Caroline Norton helped to bring about was nevertheless slow to change the attitude towards women if they were thought to have committed adultery. They were still thought to be unworthy of being a mother. In 1864 there was another much reported divorce case brought by Vice-Admiral Codrington against his wife Helen. Unlike the case of the Nortons, there was sufficient evidence to suggest that Helen Codrington had committed adultery. But what brought the case to public attention was the evidence that was brought against Helen. Halfway through the trial there was a shift when a 'sealed letter' was produced and her friend Emily Faithful testified against her. The 'sealed letter' was never opened but there was an inference that Helen and Emily had had a relationship. Whatever the true circumstances of Helen's behaviour, Admiral Codrington successfully sued for divorce and won. This case makes an important contribution to a negative image of the stepmother if she tries to put herself in the place of the mother. Helen Codrington's two daughters were immediately taken away from her, and she was never allowed to see them again. Admiral Codrington swiftly married and his daughters found themselves not only bereft of their mother, but in the care of a woman who would not allow them to mention their mother's name or write to her. Helen's letters to them were also never delivered. The stepmother literally took possession of Helen's two children and was complicit in the humiliation of Helen, thereby colluding with the popular opinion that Helen was not fit to be a mother, but at the same time leaving a dark shadow across the image of the stepmother.[33]

These two cases bring to the fore a paradoxical aspect of the sexual prejudice that has been visited upon women in general. They cannot be allowed to have equal rights to men when it comes to sexual desire. What is more silent and subtle is an insidious belief that if they were allowed equality with men then anarchy would be let loose on society, as we saw in the quotation from the Bishop of Rochester above. And so instead, it is only the stepmother who enjoys this dubious freedom; she is the seductive temptress who leads men astray and displaces or even robs the mother of her children. It is however interesting to discover that the stepmother's seductive charms are never made explicit in early transcriptions of such fairy stories as Cinderella, whereas a recent Disney rendering of Cinderella has the stepmother exuding sexually provocative behaviour towards both Cinderella and her father when they first meet.[34] This helps to reinforce the belief that the stepmother's innate cruelty is augmented by her sexuality, and it is this combination that makes her such an invincible figure, worthy of the pre-Hellenic goddesses Hera and the seductive Queen of Sheba.

There is one more characteristic that all women including the stepmother have been thought to possess that is still linked to the question of women's desire. It has been believed that they want to seduce men in order to castrate them, out of envy of men's phallic strength. Freud is said to have put it, 'The great question that has never been answered and which I have not yet been able to answer, despite my thirty years of research into the feminine soul is *Was will das Weib* [What does woman want].'[35] In spite of this disclaimer Freud did have a theory about the sexual anxieties aroused in men by the anatomical differences between the sexes. Early Freud equated shoes and slippers to symbols of female genitals[36] but then in 1927 Freud developed a new theory that shoes and slippers are not simply and straightforwardly symbols of female genitals. Shoes and slippers have now, he believes, come to represent the disavowed penis that women were believed to possess; they are a fetish. In early childhood some boys believe that girls possess penises just as they do. For these boys the realization that girls do not possess a penis arouses such anxiety that they refuse to believe this because it would mean that they might lose theirs. This becomes formulated as castration anxiety. So in adult life the slipper, for the man, becomes the comforting illusion that girls do possess a penis after all and then he can become potent.[37] This of course does not give an account of what little girls feel, except Freud imagines that they do feel themselves to be castrated boys. It is not necessary to go into all the bitter arguments that Freud's phallocentric theory has aroused amongst female psychoanalysts and other feminist writers, but it is enough to show that Freud was not unusual in imagining female sexuality and desire in terms of the male fear of castration by the envious woman who wants his penis.

Returning now to the question 'What is it that women desire?' and Freud's answer, that after thirty years of clinical work he had not been able to find the answer, I found myself wondering whether it is a question that cannot be answered, by either man or woman. It is, if you like, the wrong question. And by that I mean, implicit in that question is the idea that there is just one thing that women desire, namely sexual freedom. Maybe what underlies that question is man's wish to find a unifying and universal answer to the question of female desire. With such a thought in mind I return to the stepmother. Perhaps we shall never find one answer as to why the stepmother has always been characterized in negative terms. She is not simply a reincarnated Hera, who wishes to destroy her 'stepchildren'; nor can she be characterized as a sexually predatory Queen of Sheba, bringing incense and myrrh to the great King Solomon in order to seduce him; nor does she represent the disavowed negative feelings we have denied about the mother. She is a combination of many of these characteristics that have been used to describe all women, but with one added power. She now finds herself reincarnated in the minds of men and women as the symbol of an existential crisis. When the stepmother appears, in our fantasy our mother is no longer present or available because she has been dislodged or got rid of by the stepmother's evil machinations upon her life.

If this fantasy has any truth to it, then one of the deepest fears that men and women share is that one woman would want to take possession of another woman's position. It is not only the misogyny of men that has put women in their place and kept them down, but lurking in the background is another fear that there is no faithful solidarity amongst women. They can fight amongst themselves with as much bitterness and venom as any of the endless tales of the conflicts between the knights in the court of King Arthur.

In conclusion, I have tried to imagine the way the relationships between men and women have evolved over time, and it has been tempting to attribute many of the difficulties that the stepmother has faced to the way men have thought about and treated women more generally, and it has been easy to slip into the belief that she has become the emblematic figure of all that men most fear in women. Furthermore it is easy to get caught up in the real injustices that women have suffered such as their lack of legal and political rights and their subordination to the emotional prejudices of men. The drama of these real sufferings can lead one to forget that women also have relationships with each other. Hera may have had good reason to be angry with Zeus when he seduced Alcmene, and some of her hatred of Herakles may have been displaced anger from her powerless position with Zeus. Nevertheless her legendary behaviour towards Herakles does arouse feelings of anxiety that a woman could behave towards another woman's infant in this way. The realization that women have contributed to their own legend by their own behaviour adds another complication.

So I want to end this chapter with a final thought that, though the stepmother has had to carry some of the more deep-seated fears about women that have been projected onto her, such as beliefs about her sexually predatory nature, her innate envious and destructive character, her emotional unfaithfulness and unreliability, and her cruelty to another woman's children, we need to remember that she has at times perpetuated her own negative image, and this is particularly so when she has mistreated her stepchildren. In the words of the tale that Warner said had been written down in 1958, 'the second wife must look after the dead woman's child better than her own children.'[38]

Notes

1. Mackenzie (1917) p. xviii.
2. Mackenzie (1917) p. xlvi.
3. I thank Joe and Theo Coles for this reference. It needs to be added that this myth is to be found across many of the ancient civilizations of the world.
4. Mackenzie (1917) p. xivii and p. 186.
5. Devereux (1963) p. 207, Freud (1933), Warner (1995).
6. Blanning (2010) p. 9.
7. Harrison (2005).
8. See Homer's *The Iliad* and in particular the turmoil of the Trojan War that was perpetuated by the fighting between Zeus and Hera. 'Now Here of the Golden Throne, looking out from where she stood on the summit of Olympus, was quick to observe two things. She saw how Poseidon, who was both her Brother and her Brother-in-law, was bustling about on the field of battle, and she rejoiced. But she also saw Zeus sitting on the topmost peak of Ida of the many springs; and this sight filled the ox-eyed Lady Here with disgust' (p. 261).

9. Burkert (1985) p. 132.
10. Maddox (1975) points out that this is in fact legally inaccurate, as you are not the stepmother of your husband's illegitimate children who are born outside the marriage.
11. Burkert (1985) p. 132.
12. Burkert (1985), Harrison (2005), Mackenzie (1917).
13. Freud (1931) p. 226.
14. Jacobs (2017) p. 31.
15. Philby (1981).
16. Warner (1995) p. 97.
17. Philby (1981).
18. 1 Kings 10, *The Holy Bible*.
19. Warner (1995) p. 130.
20. Malory (2004).
21. Chaucer (1962) pp. 297–302.
22. Chaucer (1962) p. 10.
23. Chaucer (1962) p. 302.
24. See in particular Batt in Malory (2004). I am not going into the scholarly debate about the meaning of Lancelot's relationship with Guinevere.
25. Cable in Malory (1971) p. 200.
26. I am grateful to Tanya Stobbs who pointed out that Guinevere is accidentally Mordred's stepmother.
27. Castor (2005).
28. Cited in Stone (1990) p. 278.
29. Quoted in Atkinson (2012) p. 353.
30. Atkinson (2012), Cecil (1954).
31. Atkinson (2012) p. 22.
32. Stone (1990). However it was not until 1923 that a woman could sue for divorce on the basis of her husband's adultery; this was followed in 1925 by the Guardianship of Infants Act when father and mother had equal rights to custody of their children (Donoghue 2008).
33. I have taken this brief account from Donoghue (2008) and Wikipedia en.wikipedia.org and gerald-massey.org.uk.
34. *Cinderella* [film], Disney.
35. Quoted in Appignanesi and Forrester (2000) p. 2.
36. Freud (1916–1917) p. 158.
37. Freud (1927).
38. Warner (1995) p. 214.

References

Appignanesi, L. and Forrester, J. (2000) *Freud's Women*. London: Penguin Books.
Atkinson, D. (2012) *The Criminal Conversation of Mrs Norton*. London: Arrow Books.
Batt, C. (2004) Malory and Rape. In Malory, T. *Le Morte D'Arthur*. Ed. S.H.A. Shepherd. London: New York: W.W. Norton & Co.
Blanning, T. (2010) *The Romantic Revolution*. London: Phoenix.
Burkert, W. (1985) *Greek Religion*. Trans. J. Raffan. Cambridge: Harvard University Press.
Castor, H. (2005) *Blood and Roses: The Paston Family and The War of the Roses*. London: Faber & Faber.
Cecil, D. (1954) *Lord M. or The Later Life of Lord Melbourne*. London: Constable.
Chaucer, G. (1962) *The Canterbury Tales*. Trans. N. Coghill. London: Penguin Books.
Cinderella (2015) [film]. Directed by Kenneth Branagh. Walt Disney.

Donoghue, E. (2008) *The Sealed Letter*. London: Picador.
Devereux, G. (1963) The Socio-political Functions in the Oedipus Myth in Early Greece. *Psychoanalytic Quarterly.* 32: 305–214.
Freud, S. (1916–1917) Introductory Lectures on Psycho-Analysis. In *The Standard Edition of the Complete Psychological Works of Sigmund Freud. Vol. 15–16.* London: Hogarth Press. pp. 5–448.
Freud, S. (1927) Fetishism. In *The Standard Edition of the Complete Psychological Works of Sigmund Freud. Vol. 21.* London: Hogarth Press. pp. 152–159.
Freud, S. (1931) Female Sexuality. In *The Standard Edition of the Complete Psychological Works of Sigmund Freud. Vol. 21.* London: Hogarth Press. pp. 225–247.
Freud, S. (1933) New Introductory Lectures on Psycho-Analysis. In *The Standard Edition of the Complete Psychological Works of Sigmund Freud. Vol. 22.* London: Hogarth Press. pp. 7–158.
Gimbutas, M. (1991) *The Language of the Goddess.* San Francisco: Harper Collins Publishers.
Harrison, J.E. (2005) *The Religion of Ancient Greece.* London: Elibron Classics.
Homer (1950) *The Iliad.* Trans. E.V. Rieu. London: Penguin Books.
Jacobs, A. (2017) Rethinking Matricide. In *The Mother in Psychoanalysis and Beyond.* Ed. R. Mayo and C. Moutsou. London/New York: Routledge.
Mackenzie, D.A. (1917) *Crete and Pre-Hellenic Myths and Legends.* London: Gresham Publishing House.
Maddox, B. (1975) *The Half-Parent: Living with Other People's Children.* London: Andre Deutsch Ltd.
Malory, T. (1969) *The Quest of the Holy Grail.* Trans. P.M. Matarasso. London: Penguin Books.
Malory, T. (1971) *The Death of King Arthur.* Trans. J Cable. London: Penguin Books.
Malory, T. (2004) *Le Morte D'Arthur.* Ed. S.H.A. Shepherd. London/New York: W.W. Norton & Co.
Philby, H. St John (1981) *The Queen of Sheba.* London: Melbourne/New York: Quartet Books.
Plato (1955) *The Republic.* Trans. H.D.P. Lee. London: Penguin Books.
Stone, L. (1990) *The Road to Divorce.* Oxford: Oxford University Press.
The Holy Bible. Authorised Version. London: S. Bagster & Sons Ltd.
Warner, M. (1995) *From the Beast to the Blonde.* London: Vintage.

Chapter 4

The psychic moorings of a stepchild

In the last three chapters I have been concerned not only with the imaginative legacy of our fairy stories about stepmothers and to a lesser extent about fathers/stepfathers, but also with the more primordial anxiety that we have all held about powerful and older women. Here is to be found the image of the stepmother who rises like a phoenix out of the ashes of a broken marriage and is imagined to hover with malign intent upon her stepchildren. She carries the legacy of Hera, the first recorded stepmother, who had been a pagan goddess of fertility. Hera's power and her wisdom were crushed once she had been married off to Zeus. This left her, understandably, full of anger and frustration but she was powerless in the hands of this dominating god. One lasting legacy of her angry frustration with Zeus' treatment of her is that she went to alarming lengths to try and get rid of Zeus' son Herakles, who was not her own child. This unforgivable treatment of another woman's child has left us with a fearful image of the 'second mother.' Hera and her subsequent incarnations as the stepmother in our fairy stories continue to beset the life of the imagination.

I have found unfortunately that in the real world this negative image of the malign powers of the stepmother has sometimes been confirmed. The experiences that many have given of their childhood in the hands of a stepmother have reinforced the legends that she is not always a good second mother. By way of confirmation of this view I am going to explore an early literary account of a stepmother that was given by Elizabeth Gaskell (1810–1865) in her last and unfinished novel, *Wives and Daughters.* This novel weaves its way between autobiography and fiction but nevertheless gives a remarkably truthful description of the mind of the heroine of the novel, twelve-year-old Mollie, when she is presented with a stepmother. Not only that, but in minute detail Gaskell also explores the responses of the other three principal characters in this novel, Mollie's stepmother, her father and her stepsister. I have found that all these characters express feelings that are echoed in the research findings on divorcing families that one can read about today. It is for this reason that it is worth exploring Gaskell's sensitive appreciation of what can happen in a second marriage, remembering that the truth of her observation was forged upon her own experience of having a stepmother.

In 1811 Gaskell's mother had died when Elizabeth was one year old. She was the youngest of eight children, none of whom had survived except her twelve-year-old brother John, to whom she was devoted. He was drowned at sea when he was in his early twenties and Gaskell was devastated, as he was the only member of her original family who had kept constant watch and attention over her. Gaskell was sent in infancy to her mother's sister, Aunt Maud, Mrs Lumb, in Cheshire to be brought up and this was the place she considered home. Gaskell was devoted to Aunt Maud and claimed she had had a happy childhood in a lively family with innumerable cousins. In contrast her father, John Stephenson, seemed to have shown little interest in her well-being, and never visited her in Cheshire. He married again in 1814, Catherine Thompson, who was described as socially aspiring. They had two children but Mr Stephenson seemed reluctant to bring Gaskell into his new family. Eventually when Gaskell was twelve she was summoned to spend a summer with them in Chelsea. She wrote a letter many years later to a friend and said she had never been so unhappy in her life as during that visit. 'Long ago I lived in Chelsea with my father and stepmother, and *very very* unhappy I used to be; if it had not been for the beautiful, grand river, which was an inexplicable comfort to me and a family of the name of Kennett, I think my child's heart would have broken.'[1]

She not only felt that she had no deep attachment to her father, but she never felt welcomed by her stepmother. This sentiment was denied by her stepmother who wrote to Aunt Maud, at the death of Gaskell's father, 'I shall ever love Elizabeth as my own child.'[2] This self-serving letter was written when Gaskell was already nineteen and had had little to do with her father and stepmother over the years. The falsity of this stepmother's love is borne out by the fact that following the death of Gaskell's father, twenty-five years elapsed before Gaskell and her stepmother saw each other again.

Gaskell's experience of the death of her mother and the false relationship with her stepmother led her to be an ever-present and deeply concerned mother to her own children. She never wanted them to experience the loneliness she had known; and as though she was keeping up a private dialogue within herself, she kept a remarkable diary of the first year of her eldest daughter's life, in which she describes with imaginative sympathy the varying moods of her child.[3] It was not until Gaskell was in her fifties and a much respected novelist that she had the confidence and emotional distance to tackle the character of a stepmother in *Wives and Daughters*. It is interesting that it took Gaskell this length of time before she wrote about her stepmother and her father, and this seems to confirm the research work that Wallerstein (2002) and colleagues have done on the children of divorce, where they found that children of broken marriages take many more years to find a psychic equilibrium than children from intact families. We might say that Gaskell at last found an equitable perspective on herself as Molly, the heroine of her novel, and could hold a portrait of her stepmother at the distance that was necessary to show her true character. There is however one difference between the novel and Wallerstein's research. Wallerstein was optimistic that these children of divorce would eventually risk getting close to someone by their mid-thirties, whereas the challenge that Gaskell's novel poses is, does Molly find happiness in the end? Tantalizingly, we do not know how the novel was to end because Gaskell died before she had finished it.

Here are the thoughts that Molly had when her father told her he was going to marry again.

> She did not answer. She could not tell what words to use. She was afraid of saying anything, lest the passion of anger, dislike, indignation – whatever it was boiling up in her breast – should find vent in cries and screams, or worse, in raging words that could never be forgotten. It was as if the piece of solid ground on which she stood had broken from the shore, and she was drifting out to the infinite sea alone.[4]

Perhaps the most forceful image one is left with is that Molly felt 'she was drifting out to the infinite sea alone.' The idea that Molly felt untethered from all the attachments that had held her together is a dramatic image, but it holds a profound psychological truth. The child is being asked to accept and love a new person in her life who is a stranger, and who has no psychic moorings either within the child or the stepparent.[5] In tearful and indignant distress Molly continues, 'He had me. You don't know what we were to each other – at least what he was to me.'[6] Again this is a familiar response of a child when faced by a stepparent, especially if, like Molly, she and her father had lived quite happily together for eight years, following the death of Molly's mother. The question for such children is, why did the father need to marry again; surely I was enough for him? But in the face of the immutable fact of this new person disrupting the pre-existing harmony, Molly's response is a universal one. Molly inwardly accuses her father of callously forgetting the haloed image of 'her own dear mother.'[7] It is not hard to imagine how painful that thought must be for any child who loses its mother, whether through death or divorce, and finds itself confronted by a strange woman, who often insists on being called 'Maman.'

Molly finds further difficulties that follow swiftly upon the introduction of her stepmother. What is the nature of this new relationship between this strange woman and her father? This is well expressed when Molly wonders, 'how . . . [had her father] come to like Mrs Kirkpatrick [Molly's stepmother] enough to wish to marry her, [this] was an unsolved problem that she unconsciously put aside as inexplicable,' and then she falteringly had to recognize that there was 'to be a perfect confidence between these two' from which 'she [was] to be for ever shut out.'[8] One might be tempted to say that Molly is facing an Oedipal conflict that had been avoided by the earlier death of her mother. But Gaskell is too subtle a writer to reduce Molly's outrage to one explanation. Molly's suffering is complex but has similarities to the suffering of many children of divorce or those who lose their mother.

From the very beginning Molly learns that Clare (her stepmother, who was formerly Mrs Kirkpatrick) is interested only in herself. A good example is Clare's behaviour after her wedding to Molly's father, Mr Gibson. Clare calls to Molly, 'Now, my dear we can embrace each other in peace. Oh dear, how tired I am!'[9] We see in this last comment Clare's supposed concern for Molly shifts swiftly towards her own state of being. Molly is given a cursory embrace and then has to deal with Clare's exhaustion. Clare's self-concern overrides every incident and every relationship throughout the novel; whether it is about whom she will visit or how she will dress Molly or what she will say to Lord or Lady Cumnor; she is always thinking about how it will reflect best upon her self-image. Finally even Molly's father ruefully has to accept 'the fact that the wife he had chosen had a very different standard of conduct to that which he had upheld all his life and had hoped to have seen inculcated to his daughter.'[10]

Molly has no other possibility than to accept Clare's treatment of her, as indeed is the case of children who are presented with a second mother and under similar circumstances. Clare insisted that Molly should call her Mamma; then Clare dismissed Molly's nurse Betty for she felt they were too fond of each other, and the final insult was that Clare had Molly's bedroom cleared of all her mother's furniture on the pretext that it was old and outdated. The accuracy of Gaskell's observation about the devastation that Molly felt at the hand of her unimaginative stepmother is echoed all too painfully in many of the research findings on stepchildren, and in some of the accounts I have been given. Many stepmothers seem to imagine that if they wipe out the child's past attachments, a new and satisfactory life can begin.

It is hard to imagine what is going on in the mind of a stepmother who treats her stepchild with such lack of forethought. It has to be assumed that someone like Clare, Molly's stepmother, is jealous of the stepchild's past attachments. But what Clare and other stepmothers do not seem to realize is that their insensitive demands lay the foundation stone to lasting resentment on the part of their stepchild and this can lead to lasting self-doubt in the child. A child can begin to wonder, who is to be trusted? And why is my father not protecting me as he used to? Are they being treated in this way because they have done something wrong? Will anyone ever love them again if they are so bad? Molly finds it very hard to value herself or her feelings as she develops. She puts herself down and puts the needs of others, even of her stepmother, before her own wishes. I believe that in the end we are left with the fear that she cannot imagine she might be lovable.

Gaskell's comments about this fictional account of a second marriage reflect another truth that is confirmed by many research findings; second marriages are frequently unstable. Clare does not find the social satisfaction she had hoped for when she married Mr Gibson, Mr Gibson is irritated by Clare's social aspirations and Molly feels unloved and ignored. Gaskell's truthful observation about the vulnerability of second marriages is confirmed by the US National Center for Health Statistics who reported that 'one half of those marrying in the 1990s were getting married for the second time.'[11] One reason for the vulnerability of second marriages is beautifully reflected in this novel. Clare and Mr Gibson are unable to think beyond their own passionate needs. Mr Gibson thought that he could not deal with Molly's burgeoning sexual attractiveness to young men. He imagined that if he married again his new wife would deal with these matters. Mrs Kirkpatrick wanted to marry again, as her age and her failing looks were beginning to threaten her with a solitary life. Neither of them had sympathy for the emotional needs of the other, or of their children. Clare is incapable of reflecting upon her own behaviour and so she is unable to imagine that Mr Gibson's gradual exasperation with her might have anything to do with her behaviour. Mr Gibson, in his turn, is also not given to self-reflection; in his mind it leads into uncharted places that are better left undisturbed and so he never speaks about his disappointment and irritation. It is this failure of empathy towards the other's state of mind and a lack of self-reflection that leads many second marriages into the same place as the previous marriage.

When Molly wonders how it was possible for her father to like her stepmother there was some truth in her perception. In the end their marriage was a disappointment to them all, confirming the statistics that second marriages often fail to bring the expected happiness. Molly's prescient question 'how had he come to like [her] enough to marry her'[12] revealed an unhappy truth; Mr Gibson and Clare Kirkpatrick did not like each other enough to make a satisfactory second marriage. They were marrying an image of the person they wanted, not the person they actually married. Molly's reflection picks up more than Oedipal outrage; she had intuitively picked up the tenuous nature of this second marriage.

There is another anxiety that children may be expressing when they believe that a second marriage is a mistake. Gaskell skilfully wove into her novel the largely unconscious anxiety about the power and meaning of sex and sexual desire for a pre-pubescent child as it witnesses the excitement engendered by a parent forming a new marriage. Mr Gibson was himself confused about his sexual feelings. He began to think about the need for a new wife when he was overwhelmed by uncomfortable feelings about Molly's burgeoning sexuality and his dawning awareness of his jealousy that one day she would fall in love with a man and leave him. He could not face that and preferred to believe that if he had a second wife she would deal with this matter, and by implication, his own uncomfortable feelings. But what he had not realized, until too late, was that the woman he married was ill equipped to help Molly move into adolescence. Clare was always looking for confirmation of her own sexual attractiveness and needed to obscure Molly and her needs. It is not hard to imagine that what Molly found perturbing was the sexual atmosphere between her father and stepmother. A new sexual excitement frequently enters into a second marriage, and it can become especially difficult, as in the case of twelve-year-old Molly, when a daughter of the first marriage is just entering puberty. It disrupts the development of her own sexual feelings. Gaskell has a masterly understanding of the disquiet to a pre-pubescent daughter if suddenly the adults are sporting their sexuality for all to see. She has Molly repudiate her own growing desires and has her imagine that she has nothing but brotherly love for any young man she encounters. Many children like Molly can find the new intrusion of adult sexual desire as purposively tantalizing and it is reported that many children brought into the newly created second home listen at the door of the new marital bedroom.[13]

Gaskell's capacity to give voice to the complexity of Molly's feelings about her father's remarriage and about her stepmother makes it a novel of extraordinary psychological insight. But Gaskell is not content to give her sole attention to the unfolding drama of Molly's relationship with her stepmother and her father; there is another stepchild in the tale who suffers perhaps even more. Molly discovers she has a stepsibling, Cynthia, who was the child of Clare and her first husband who had died when Cynthia was four. At that point Cynthia had been sent off to boarding school and had scarcely seen her mother since. Molly finds in Cynthia a companion for whom she can feel compassion, especially when Cynthia, with brutal honesty, says she can never forgive her mother for her neglect. But the profound maternal neglect that Cynthia suffered leaves Cynthia with little recourse but to excite the sympathy of men, as she develops into an unusually beautiful young woman. She is in danger of becoming pregnant in order to give herself some emotional hold on life; in Cynthia's case she becomes secretly engaged to a man who proceeds to blackmail her.

Cynthia's seductiveness is given another twist as she tries to find a place in her new family. She finds herself, eventually, taken into the Gibson household and is delighted to find she has a stepfather. We discover that she had been kept safely out of the way of her mother for many years lest her beauty attract the attention of a man that her mother was fancying. Not surprisingly, when Cynthia finds herself beside Mr Gibson, she is desperate to find favour with him. However she soon found that she did not stand a chance in comparison to his daughter Molly. Mr Gibson had brought up his daughter to be truthful, at whatever cost, whereas Cynthia had had to dissimulate throughout her short life in order to survive her loneliness. She was able to attract the attention of men while never trusting anyone. Mr Gibson was both sympathetic to her charms but dismayed by her capacity to dissociate from the truth of a situation. The ultimate tragedy for Cynthia, and it is to be found in much research on stepchildren, was that however hard she tried to gain Mr Gibson's whole-hearted love and attention she inevitably failed. It is indeed difficult to imagine that any man or woman might prefer a stepchild rather than their own biological child. Over and over again the evidence points to the fact that it is rare for stepparents to feel as devoted to their stepchildren as to their own children. And it is equally rare to find a child saying that a stepparent has been a better parent than their own, whatever the circumstances. So yet again Gaskell imaginatively shows us the heart of a stepdaughter who encounters a stepfather who cannot give her the untrammelled admiration of a father whom she has searched for all her life. She is left heartbroken.

In this novel Gaskell has given us a compelling account of the vicissitudes of a second marriage. All the four characters that play a part in this second family, Molly, her father, her stepmother Clare and her stepsibling Cynthia, suffer from unwelcome intrusions and unmet expectations and hopes, and in the closing pages of the novel we are left with a desolate image. Molly has yearned for love and attention from a suitable man and throughout the novel the figure of Roger hovers sympathetically, but she cannot imagine that he might love her. As the novel draws to the end Molly is able to recognize that she has always loved Roger though she has been at pains to deny this fact. It gradually dawns on Roger also that Molly has many qualities that he admires and loves, however he has to leave the country to do further research. He comes to say goodbye to Molly, but nothing can be said between them because Clare is also present. As he leaves he stands outside the house and looks back towards the window where both Molly and Clare are standing. Molly waves a white handkerchief, 'yet she is not sure if he perceived her modest quiet movement, for Mrs Gibson (Molly's stepmother) became immediately so demonstrative that Molly fancied that her eager foolish pantomimic motions must absorb all his attentions.'[14] The anxiety Molly felt, that Roger the man she loved might not have seen her wave, describes well the psychological damage a foolish and intrusive stepmother can do to a stepchild. Such a stepmother can so intrude upon her stepchild that the internal images of the loving presence of another are constantly being pushed aside.[15] Molly's doubts about Roger's love are on the periphery of her psychic vision as she and her stepmother wave at him from the window. How could she be sure he really loved her? Has he noticed her wave? And at the end of story I am left with the fear that for Molly such a person as Roger will always be in danger of becoming a fleeting figure, forever going 'abroad.' She can never be quite sure that she is worthy of love with the result that when other demands are made upon her she will feel obliged to attend to them rather than her own.

I chose Gaskell's novel, *Wives and Daughters*, as I was struck by her truthful insights into the mind of a young girl as she moved into adolescence and had at the same time to witness her father trying to establish a new and sexual relationship with a woman she did not know. It could be said that Gaskell's imaginative grasp of Molly's mind is in contrast to her own stable life, with her devotion to her husband and her children. But when she died, with this unfinished novel in her hands, she was concealing a secret from her husband. She had just bought what she hoped would be her dream holiday house in Hampshire, for herself and her husband when he retired from being a Unitarian minister in Manchester. Throughout her married life she had longed to live in the country away from the bad drains of the city but her husband was totally committed to his work. In the end, with the help from her daughters and her two sons-in-law, she bought a house in Alton in Hampshire. She kept it secret from her husband not least because she had had to buy it on a mortgage, which he would have abhorred. She hoped to tell him about their retirement home when she had paid off her debts through finishing *Wives and Daughters*. This was not to be because on the afternoon when the house was finally completed and all her family were present, except her husband and one of her daughters who was looking after him and concealing where the rest of the family were, she was sitting in her armchair after lunch and peacefully died of heart failure. What was significant about her sudden death was that her husband knew nothing about where she was or what she had done. It was this fact that made me wonder whether Molly waving her handkerchief at the window to a vanishing figure was not expressing an unattainable longing in Gaskell's own heart.

It is with the image of heartbreak that I am going to return to the central emotional conflict that Molly faced when she was told by her father that he was going to marry again. I want to do this bearing in mind some of the research literature on the consequences of a second marriage upon children and the comments I have been given by people whom I have interviewed about their stepparents. Molly was first of all outraged as the fantasy that she and her father could live for the rest of their lives in perfect harmony was shattered. This wish has similarities to the moment of conflict in the fairy story of 'Donkey-Skin' when a widowed father and daughter are confronted by the daughter's sexual attractiveness. This is an especially vulnerable moment if there is no mother around to take the father's attention away from his daughter and a father and daughter can slip into dangerous incestuous waters. The daughter needs to know that her fantasy of a perfect life together with her father is no more than a dream, however unpleasant that realization might be. One might say that a stepmother is much needed at this moment to break up this dream, but as legend and real life experience so painfully show, she is often not up to the task of being a loving second mother.

The next dilemma that Molly had to face was that she was excluded from a new intimacy that she was merely called upon to witness. She puzzled as to what her father could have seen in her stepmother Clare. There is more to this question than just Oedipal fury or narcissistic rage. In the child's belief that this second marriage was a mistake, there may indeed be an intuitive sense in the child's mind that the foundation of this new marriage is rocky. Here I want to bring in an account of a man I interviewed, who, like Molly, could not understand what his father saw in his second wife, his stepmother. His parents divorced just as he was leaving home and starting on a sexual relationship himself. He believed that this second marriage was a mistake, and he still held passionately to this belief, thirty years later. He could not imagine what his father saw in this woman whose way of life and values were so at variance with those that he had come to respect in his father. His stepmother seemed to him to be unforgivably like Clare Gibson, Molly's stepmother. She was insensitive to her stepson and jealous of his relationship with his father. She did not want him coming to the house and tried to disparage the father's previous marriage. Not surprisingly this man has a lasting contempt for his stepmother.

I want to suggest that the belief that one's parent's second marriage is a mistake carries a lot more meaning than the word implies.[16] The idea of a mistake, in these circumstances, is linked to the child witnessing a 'shadow' that is revealed when seeing a parent attempting a new relationship. Suddenly, as this man said, the values that he so much admired in his father were shattered. But what were these values that had been shattered? I think one answer might be that he wished his father could keep his sexual desires private and ideally confined to the marital bed.

But instead, his father revealed a side of himself that to his son was most disrupting, namely his sexuality. It was as though the father had to have a new mate in competition with his son. This had also been the reason that Mr Gibson, Molly's father, had decided to marry again. He could not bear to think that he might lose his daughter to a younger man. When adolescent or slightly older children, whose parents break up, believe that the parents have made a mistake, they may be talking about a 'shadow' that has fallen upon their fantasies surrounding their own burgeoning sexuality and this can throw their sexual development into disarray, so that they become sexually inhibited or sexually promiscuous.

We have learned a lot from psychoanalytic theory about the early sexual fantasies of children in terms of the Oedipus complex, but there has been much more reluctance to acknowledge that parents can be sexually jealous of their children. One consequence has been that parents are surprisingly unaware of what might be impelling them to seek a new mate at just the moment when they are faced with their child's sexual potential, such as was the case of Mr Gibson. There can be an unconscious compulsion on the part of the adult to change partners at such a moment. The truth of such a thought was borne out by a man I interviewed who left his wife at the same time as his daughter was leaving for university. He said, 'I never felt satisfied sexually by my wife, and I realized that if I did not search for satisfaction now I might never have the experience before it was too late.' What parents can forget is that if they leave home just at the time their children are also leaving home and seeking sexual partners they can leave behind a trail of sexual conflict in their children. An awareness of the newly married couple's sexuality may be precociously forced upon the child at a time when the child needs room to find a place for its own desires. This intrusiveness of adult sexuality into the psychic imagination of a young girl like Molly, or even into the experience of the man I interviewed above, is almost as invasive as pornography and one consequence can be that they wish to repudiate all thoughts of sexual desire, their own or that of their parents with their new partners.[17] No wonder they hate the intruder who brings these unwelcomed or one might say premature messages. In the case of Molly, her own burgeoning sexuality took a knock from which she never fully recovered, and one consequence was that she found it almost impossible to imagine she might excite the desires of a man.

When parents divorce, whatever age their children may be, their children spend the rest of their lives with the silent hope that their parents might get back together again. This yearning imposes itself in different fantasies at different ages but the important point is that it takes up a lot of a child's emotional energy as it imagines ways of bringing its parents together again, whether at a school occasion or family party. This longing that the parents should reunite robs the child of the much needed space for its own fantasies and desires, and this suggests that the need for a united family seems as fundamental to our psychic well-being as any contrary Oedipal wish to divide them.

The premature messages about adult sexual desire that are forced upon children whose parents separate have other consequences as well. Not all children, like Molly, repudiate their own burgeoning excitement; on the contrary many girls from broken homes become sexually promiscuous at an early age and teenage pregnancies are more common among such girls.[18] How many teenage mothers have said 'I wanted a child so that I would have someone who would love me'; and that is surely the desperate note of a child who feels unnoticed by the adults who themselves are absorbed in the search for someone to love. Wallerstein and her colleagues chart very well the inevitable loss of attention and concern for the children as parents break up. The parents are in the midst of sorting out their own emotional crises and have little psychic space for their children, and this is the moment when their children, especially in early adolescence, can feel they are falling through the net, or drifting out to sea, as no one is thinking about them.

When Molly felt 'she was drifting out to the infinite sea alone' there are other images that are conjured up, in particular her belief that the old values that had secured her safety are felt to have been thrown overboard. This finds its symbolic expression when her stepmother throws out her mother's furniture. Similarly the man I interviewed above had to listen to his stepmother deriding the past and disparaging his father's relationship with his mother. Another woman whom I interviewed told me that when her father married again, her beloved nurse was dismissed because she was told she would never become attached to her stepmother if the nurse remained. It is at times almost unbearable to think of what children suffer when all their safety nets are cast adrift.

There are several conclusions I want to draw from the portrait of the stepchild I have encountered in this chapter. I am left with an image of Molly Gibson, who I imagined had been left with well-subdued feelings of anger and distrust that could only be expressed in unobtrusive ways. She would never want to disturb anyone, so she would always have to wave her handkerchief, to signal her existence, and in a way that was not noticed by those whom it might offend. I have also been left with an image of her strength and the belief that whatever her suffering she would never completely turn her back on life. Nevertheless we live today in a society where almost half of our children come from divorced families.[19] It is a painful fact but all the research evidence suggests these children are emotionally hurt by divorce. The contentious issue is whether this damage can be healed well enough so the wound does not open up again when adult life proves difficult. I have come to the conclusion that it would be a mistake to think that 'divorce is a transient crisis' and that children will recover from the trauma.[20] They are changed for life though some may survive better than others.

Notes

1 I have based my account of Gaskell's life from her biography written by W. Gérin (1976).
2 Gérin (1976) p. 38.
3 Gérin (1976) p. 54. *My Diary* was privately printed by Clement Shorter, London in 1923.
4 Gaskell (1866) p. 111 (1996).

5   Wallerstein and Lewis (2007) p. 457.
6   Gaskell (1866) p. 116.
7   Gaskell (1866) p. 114.
8   Gaskell (1866) pp. 126–134.
9   Gaskell (1866) p. 172.
10 Gaskell (1866) p. 386.
11 Wallerstein et al. (2002) note p. 256.
12 Gaskell (1866) p. 127.
13 Gaskell (1866) p. 134.
14 Wallerstein et al. (2002).
15 Gaskell (1866) p. 645.
16 At the time of writing this I read Colm Tóibín's article on Joyce's *Portrait of the Artist as a Young Man*. I was struck by a passage in which Joyce railed against an English Jesuit and ended his diatribe with the following sentence, 'My soul frets in the shadow of his language' (*Guardian Review*, 31 December 2016).
17 The distinction I am making here is that when parents divorce and seek new sexual partners their sexual desires are made transparent to their children and stepchildren, and this can feel very intrusive. Mary Shelley expressed this well in her rage against her father in her novel *Mathilda* (see Chapter 5).
18 The UK has the highest teenage pregnancy rate of any other country in Europe, though it is now at an all-time low. Statistically teenage pregnancy is linked to poverty, low educational attainment and broken family structure. See also the ACE (2015) report: cph.org.uk/wp-content/uploads/2016/01/ACE-Report-FINAL-E.pdf.
19 The divorce rate of a first marriage is well over 50 per cent and it most frequently occurs between the fourth and eighth year of marriage (Leach 2014 p. xv).
20 Wallerstein et al. (2002) p. 23, also Leach (2014).

References

Gaskell, E. (1966 [1866]) *Wives and Daughters*. London: Penguin Books.
Gérin, W. (1976) *Elizabeth Gaskell: A Biography*. Oxford: Oxford University Press.
Joyce, J. (1916) *A Portrait of the Artist as a Young Man*. London: Penguin Books.
Leach, P. (2014) *Family Breakdown: Helping Children to Hang on to Both Their Parents*. London: Unbound.
Shelley, M. (2013) *Mathilda and Other Stories*. Introduction and Notes J. DiPlacid. Ware: Wordsworth Classics.
Tóibín, C. (2016) 'What happened to us all?' In *Guardian Review* (31 December 2016).
Wallerstein, J., Lewis J. and Blakeslee, S. (2002) *The Unexpected Legacy of Divorce: A 25 Year Landmark Study*. London: Fusion Press.
Wallerstein, J. and Lewis, J.M. (2007) Sibling Outcomes and Disparate Parenting and Stepparenting After Divorce: Report From a 10-Year Longitudinal Study. *Psychoanalytic Psychology*. 24: 445–458.

Chapter 5
No longer the fairy tale stepmother

I have been pursuing the idea, in the first three chapters, that the image we have of the stepmother has been unfairly weighted against her through the imaginative impact of our fairy stories and our cultural myths. However that is only partly true. In the fictional account of Molly's stepmother we have one who is insensitive and inept. There are unfortunately other non-fictional cases where the stepmother has been as cruel as her counterpart in the fairy story, and I am going to consider one such case in this chapter. I have chosen this stepmother because she seems to have many of the same characteristics as described in Cinderella and furthermore there is a father who does not step in to protect his daughter and there are destructive sibling conflicts between the stepchildren. The stepmother was Mary-Jane Clairmont (1768–1841), the father was William Godwin (1756–1836), and the three stepsisters[1] were Fanny Imlay (1794–1816), Mary Godwin (1797–1851) (whom I shall now refer to by her well-known name of Mary Shelley) and Jane Clairmont (1798–1879).

I shall begin with Mary Shelley, first, because, like Cinderella, she believed she had escaped from her unhappy home and had managed to find her prince, Percy Bysshe Shelley. We might almost be tempted to believe, as we follow her married life, through her subsequent experience of her father's treatment of her, that her life has some of the hallmarks of the sequel to Cinderella, namely Donkey-Skin. Mary Shelley's life began in 1797 with the death of her mother, Mary Wollstonecraft (1759–1797), following the familiar puerperal fever that could accompany the unhygienic care of women in childbirth. This is the familiar background to many of our fairy stories in which the mother dies and leaves a child to its subsequent traumatic fate. Mary Shelley's mother, Mary Wollstonecraft, was married to William Godwin. They were a formidable pair and two of the best-known radical philosophers of their day, indeed they were probably the voice of the radical left.[2] Wollstonecraft had written *Vindication of the Rights of Woman* (1792) in response to the stirrings of the French Revolution, and Godwin's *Political Justice* (1793) challenged some of the fundamental institutional structures of society, such as marriage and the church. But their short-lived marriage came to an end at Mary Shelley's birth.

From the moment of Wollstonecraft's death Godwin's life was changed dramatically and his status as a radical thinker underwent an unwelcome shift. The principal reason for the change in public respect for Godwin followed from the *Memoirs* (1798) he published after Wollstonecraft's death. Godwin imagined that a truthful account of their love affair, Wollstonecraft's pregnancy with his child and their later marriage, would soothe his pain and remind the world of his wife's unique gifts. But in revealing the truth about her life with him he also revealed her earlier life with Gilbert Imlay by whom she had had an illegitimate child, Fanny. The revelation about her two pregnancies outside wedlock did much damage to Wollstonecraft's reputation. She was already a woman whose ideas did not find favour with the conservative thinkers of her time, especially those who had political power and wealth. They were fearful that an English Revolution was imminent and her book had done nothing to allay their fears. It seemed that Godwin's *Memoirs* was a further proof that the morals of these radical thinkers could not be trusted. Here was the most popular left wing philosopher of the day not only describing a relationship with a woman of dubious moral standards, a 'lascivious whore,'[3] but, who, in the course of this relationship, had also turned his back on one of his main radical ideas; he had succumbed to social pressure and married, against all his rational principles. He was thought to have provided an example of the very ingredients that had given rise to the French Revolution, untrustworthiness.

This sketch of Mary Shelley's parents' thinking and way of life is necessary if we are to try and understand some of the conflicting passions that assailed her about her father, her stepmother, marriage and the way to lead her life. Mary's most intense relationship was with her father, who, in his turn, adored her and took her every day to visit her mother's gravestone in St Pancras Church graveyard.[4] They became the emotional centre of each other's life, though by today's standards we might think he was too stringent in his demands upon her; she was to fulfil her intellectual potential with constant study and she was never to disturb him when he was working or make a noise elsewhere in the house. Added to these stringent demands he was never able to show her warm physical affection by taking her on his knee.[5]

The first four years of Mary Shelley's life were affected by her mother's death but also by the public reaction to Godwin's book about her mother. Everywhere Godwin went he was reviled and his proposals of marriage to at least two women were turned down. But at last one woman did appear who wanted him and this was Mary-Jane Clairmont, who in 1801 moved in next door to Godwin and set about seducing him. He was flattered and captivated and seemingly unaware that her over-riding motive was to marry him and become an accepted member of society. She had had two illegitimate children, Charles aged seven and Jane aged three, and was desperate to find a husband to rescue her from living on the outer edges of respectability. There was a popular account of Mary-Jane's well laid plan to catch Godwin, which one biographer, St Clair (1989), believes was a later and unkind comment upon her. One day she saw Godwin standing on the balcony of his house and she called out, 'Is it possible that I behold the immortal Godwin?' and when he assented, she replied, 'You great being, how I adore you!'[6] True or not, she did find a way of getting herself into his bed and when she became pregnant she and her family moved into his home and he married her.

There is general agreement in all the biographical accounts I have read that Mary-Jane Clairmont was a 'wicked' stepmother to her stepdaughter.[7] She was a difficult woman whose most unfortunate characteristic was her need to lie about almost everything. Not only did she need to lie but her troubled life spilled out into her everyday encounters with the world. It was said she needed to deceive the world about her assumed aristocratic origins so she wore 'green-tinted spectacles like Robespierre'![8] But unlike Robespierre her reign of terror did not come to a sudden end. Instead she ruled the Godwin household with 'an ugly temper and made scenes in public when she felt slighted, which was often.' Godwin was moved to counsel her, 'Manage and economise your temper' as she slammed doors and had temper tantrums if she could not get her own way, and, he added, 'suppress in part the excesses of that baby sullenness to be brought out every day for every trifle.'[9]

It is Mary-Jane's treatment of Mary Shelley and Mary Shelley's half-sister Fanny Imlay that is heartrending and is worth dwelling upon further, because here one can see how her insensitive and inept behaviour towards her two stepchildren does serve to reinforce the popular opinion that stepmothers are wicked. Once she had settled in to the Godwin household, and one might add, got her way, she began to assert her power and authority over her two stepchildren, Fanny, aged seven, and Mary aged four. She had a violent temper and so she would smack them when in a fury and this was a profound shock to both Fanny and Mary who had never known any uncontrolled violence.[10] Not only were they visited with Mary-Jane's temper but Mary-Jane immediately sacked their nurses, Marguerite and Linda, whom they had known from early childhood. As if this was not enough she then insisted that Fanny and Mary call her 'Mamma.' Mary always refused. Tragically the more fragile Fanny could not find a satisfactory place within this new family and slipped into a long-lasting depression. In her early twenties she killed herself, leaving behind a note saying that she believed her birth had been 'unfortunate' and one result had been that she had been a cause of 'pain to those' who had looked after her.[11]

Many of Godwin's friends were appalled as they witnessed Mary-Jane's treatment of her stepchildren. One of the most venomous descriptions of her was penned by Charles Lamb, who called her 'a bitch,'[12] and there was another popular belief that Coleridge's poem *Christabel* was a covert description of her, even though it had been written before Mary-Jane had appeared in Godwin's life. Within Godwin's family and his circle of friends, she was not a welcome addition.[13]

It would be convenient to link Mary-Jane's need to dominate and control her stepdaughter with Mary Shelley's subsequent impulsive elopement with Percy Bysshe Shelley (1792–1822) when she was no more than sixteen. But Mary Shelley's unhappiness had been forged by the death of her mother at her birth and so Mary-Jane's entrance inevitably served to highlight Mary's vulnerability and enhanced a clash that is all too familiar between stepmothers and stepchildren. Mary was an intelligent and strong-willed stepdaughter who had been openly adored by her father and by those who looked after her, and now she found herself being dominated by a powerful stepmother who resented Mary's place in the family. It is therefore not surprising that Mary held a lasting resentment that her stepmother had taken her father away from her, a well-known feature in many stepfamilies. Mary felt humiliated as she watched Godwin physically embrace his new wife, when she had known little physical tenderness from him herself. Furthermore Godwin's betrayal of Mary was compounded, in her mind, by his obliviousness to the tensions between herself and Mary-Jane. He never took his daughter's part when Mary-Jane was trying to break Mary's will, nor when Mary was being accused of having corrupted her stepsister Jane Clairmont.

As the years went on Mary Shelley's distress and fury began to express itself through chronic eczema. She was sent off to boarding school but this made no difference. Finally, when Mary was in her early teens, Godwin, in fury and despair about his recalcitrant daughter, sent her to Scotland to a widower, William Baxter, who had four daughters. Godwin did not know this man, but knew this man admired his ideas. This was enough to secure Godwin's belief that Mary would be looked after well enough. In fact it turned out to be a life-transforming moment for her. She got on well with his four daughters and as they freely roamed the Scottish hills around Dundee, she found freedom and a love of the wildness of the place that allowed her imagination to develop and her eczema left her forever. We shall see how this Scottish landscape returns in her novel *Mathilda* that will be considered at the end of the chapter.

The Godwin household was not a happy home for the children that lived there. The tensions were undoubtedly fuelled by the conflicts between stepmother and stepdaughter, but what added to the poisonous atmosphere was Mary-Jane's envy of the Godwin and Wollstonecraft inheritance that her stepdaughter Mary Shelley possessed. Mary Shelley was delicate and beautiful and her intelligence outshone that of Mary-Jane's daughter, Jane Clairmont. How could this envious stepmother rise above the shadow of Godwin's first wife, Mary Wollstonecraft? Mary-Jane knew she would never be treated with the veneration she might have liked nor gain the respect of Wollstonecraft's children. This must surely be the lot of many stepmothers who replace a much more remarkable mother; in comparison she knew she had failed and that Godwin's short-lived marriage had left him with an idealized image of his dead wife that she could never hope to supersede. And as if to remind her of this fact, she faced Mary Wollstonecraft's portrait every day as it hung over Godwin's mantelpiece.[14]

Mary-Jane was further disillusioned by her marriage to 'the immortal Godwin' when she discovered that they were always chronically short of money. She stormed out of the marriage on several occasions, sometimes for several weeks, sometimes for no more than hours or days, when Godwin's debts mounted.[15] How many unsupported women with children have imagined there would be financial security once they married, only to find that the man they married was financially inept? And it was poverty that Mary-Jane most dreaded. She had twice spent time in a debtors' prison before she had married Godwin.

If it is hard to like Mary-Jane one can admire her capacity to keep going. At the height of their insolvency she persuaded Godwin to start a bookshop, M-J Godwin & Co, which had the subsidiary title of Juvenile Library, and for many years she worked behind the counter selling children's books. M-J Godwin & Co was not only a bookshop but it was also a publishing house for some of her own and Godwin's children's stories, as well as famously publishing Charles and Mary Lamb's *Tales from Shakespeare*. The Godwin Juvenile Library is a fascinating footnote to the change that was taking place in the nineteenth century when the idea of publishing children's literature became a commercial possibility. We saw in the previous chapters that the Grimm Brothers had begun to publish their collection of folk stories to great commercial acclaim in 1812. And here, in 1805, was an enterprising woman imagining the possibility of making money out of publishing children's stories. The bookshop and publishing house is also a good example of the subtle way in which the recognition of children's imaginative and educational needs was being woven into the fabric of the moral values of the society. For instance, Godwin wrote moral tales for children but he did not dare publish them under his own name lest they be read as radical and subversive literature.[16] Mary-Jane's fortitude in the face of Godwin's total incapacity to manage the family finances may have saved the family from the debtors' prison, but it fuelled Mary Shelley's resentment even further when she was expected to work in the shop. She was not exactly the Cinderella in the ashes, but she was certainly the resentful stepdaughter who might have imagined her mother would never have asked her to do such a thing.

It seems clear that there was little that was creative and positive in the relationship between Mary-Jane and Mary Shelley and this failed relationship was augmented by Godwin's inattention to what was going on. In many ways he was a representation of Cinderella's father. He absented himself from the family as he immersed himself in his work and seems to have been unable to confront his wife and protect his two daughters.[17] And one consequence was, as in the fairy story, the three stepsisters became enmeshed in relationships between themselves that left them all bruised and mutilated. The three stepsisters, Fanny Imlay, Mary Shelley and Jane Clairmont, could never trust each other, and here we find a psychological truth in the Cinderella fairy story that is matched in real life in the Godwin family; warring stepchildren are bred in the atmosphere of parental failure. The Godwin stepchildren were full of angry dissension amongst themselves that led to tragic consequences for them all and no one lived happily ever after with a prince, in spite of Mary's hope that Shelley would turn out to be one.

Fanny Imlay's life was the most tragic of them all. She was three years old when her mother, Mary Wollstonecraft, died and she was plunged into a life with a man she scarcely knew, though she did have her nurse Marguerite to look after her until Mary-Jane came along and dismissed her. She soon discovered that

Godwin was always irritated by her, not least because she was not as attractive physically as Mary and she did not match up to his ideal image of her mother. When she was twelve Godwin told her he was not her father and this crushed her faltering self-esteem. She became even more deeply depressed as she failed to court the attention of either of her stepparents, though her need to remain as a 'good' child persisted throughout her short life. One result of her desperate need to be noticed by a parental figure was that she was never trusted as a loyal friend by either of her female stepsiblings. For instance, when Mary had fallen in love with Shelley and she was planning to elope with him, Fanny could not be trusted with this plan, lest she tell her stepparents.

By contrast, Jane Clairmont, Mary-Jane's three-year-old daughter, had a complicated but different experience when she entered the Godwin household. Unlike the depressed Fanny or the quiet and studious Mary, she was described at this time as a 'sullen, dark little brunette with speaking black eyes' who was 'her mother's darling and had many of her ways,' that is to say her moods were as tempestuous as those of her mother. She resented Mary and Mary's devotion to her father and at the same time 'resented Mary's private contempt for her mother.' This led to Jane developing 'an ambivalent fixation on . . . [Mary] that Mary never found a way to live with comfortably or to escape.'[18]

It is difficult to summarize the complex relationship between Mary Shelley and Jane Clairmont. (Jane later on changed her name to Claire and so from now on I shall refer to her as Claire.) But it would be true to say that Claire's feeling of inferiority, that she experienced the moment she stepped into the Godwin household, led her to spend the rest of her life searching for an identity in which she would feel less envious of Mary.[19] However the way she set about it led in the end to the destruction of all the important relationships in her life.

Perhaps the most important example of Claire's destructive envy of Mary is woven into Mary's relationship with Shelley. When Mary was sixteen and had returned from her Scottish sojourn, she found Shelley and her father had become very friendly, and Shelley visited Godwin most days. Mary and Shelley fell in love but this was untenable because Shelley was already married with a child. However, accompanied by Claire they could take illicit walks and plan their elopement. When it was decided that Mary and Shelley would elope, Claire willingly went with them to Europe. Their first adventure was not successful and they ran out of money and returned within six weeks. By this time Mary was pregnant and desperately sick and she withdrew from Shelley. Claire and Shelley were often on their own as Mary lay in bed and there is evidence that they became lovers. There followed a tempestuous denouement between the two stepsisters and Claire left the ménage for several months.[20] The break with Mary and Shelley led Claire to attempt a separate life in London where she became the lover of Byron and pregnant with his child Allegra. However Byron wanted nothing to do with her, so she returned to Mary and Shelley and was accepted back into what was to become from now on a *ménage à trois*. All three of them publicly announced that Allegra had been adopted but that did not save them from being popularly called 'The League of Incest.'[21] It is not necessary to go into all the details of the tragic life of Claire's daughter Allegra, but one thing was certain, Claire loved her passionately and never recovered from Allegra's early death when Allegra was handed over to Byron's care.

There was some truth in the label all three of them were given, 'The League of Incest,' as there is not only evidence that Claire and Shelley may have had an affair when Mary became so ill during her first pregnancy, but there are letters from Shelley to Claire during the last years of Shelley's life, suggestive of his love and need for Claire that she willingly gave him. They reveal an intimacy that Shelley no longer shared with Mary and Holmes finds convincing evidence that at this time Claire miscarried Shelley's child.[22] But Claire remained to all intents and purposes an 'ugly sister' to Cinderella. She mutilated her own future by seducing Byron and having an illegitimate child and then she gained the dubious reward of the secret love of her stepsister's husband. After Shelley's death she spent the rest of her life in Europe, sometimes as a governess, lonely and embittered.[23]

For Mary Shelley, both her stepsisters caused her conflict and suffering. She was never able to develop a close relationship with Fanny even though they shared the same mother; their relationship was not helped by Godwin's admiration for Mary and his belief that she was Wollstonecraft's true daughter, both intellectually and physically, while subtly making Fanny feel she was not worthy to be her mother's daughter. With Claire it was different and more difficult. Mary always felt uneasy in her presence. They were, in the first instance, temperamentally unsuited; Mary was quiet and withdrawn and only expressed her anger somatically, such as developing chronic eczema, whereas Claire was volatile and erratic, like her mother, given to moods and deeply conflicted by her mother's hatred of Mary. In the early heady days of Mary's romance with Shelley, Mary was grateful for Claire's willingness to further the illicit courtship. Indeed it is probably true that without Claire's help, Mary and Shelley may never have succeeded in eloping. But it became clear, quite early on, that Claire also wanted Shelley's attention and when Mary was ill throughout her first pregnancy, Claire was only too willing to become Shelley's companion. There are painful letters, during this time, that Mary wrote to Shelley saying she could not support Claire's presence any longer; '*absentia Clairiae*' she wrote on several occasions.[24] However once Claire was pregnant with Byron's child and reviled by him, Mary's kindness prevailed and she accepted Claire back into the ménage and welcomed Claire's child Allegra. But the stepsiblings never really trusted each other. When Shelley died Mary returned to England, thankful to be without Claire, but their relationship did not end there. Claire threatened to return to England to live with Mary, and this provoked Mary, in 1836, to summarise her own feelings about Claire: 'we were never friends . . . she poisoned my life when young . . . she had still the faculty of making me more uncomfortable than any human being . . . a faculty she . . . never fails to exert.'[25] The difficulty that all these stepsiblings shared was deep seated and extended beyond the rough and tumble of sibling love and hate. As in the

Cinderella fairy story, their envious rivalry was fuelled by the stepmother's hatred of her stepchildren. A telling phrase about Mary-Jane, written by Mary Shelley, likened her to a storm at sea, 'an evil stepmother [who] deceives and betrays all committed to her care,'[26] and this fundamental betrayal of maternal care lay at the heart of the stepsiblings' difficulties. It seems that Mary-Jane found pleasure in stirring up discord and discontent within the family; in the words of Muriel Spark, she was a woman who 'felt her inferiority and in her muddled way compensated by doing all the damage she could.'[27] Her envy and jealousy added to an inevitable tension that arises between stepsiblings as they try to get to know each other and build up a relationship. It is commonplace for stepsiblings to feel that they are hated intruders and it takes great parental skill to gradually modulate the initial reaction of these children who are strangers to each other. But where both parents are unwilling or unable to sort out these early quarrels, as was clearly the case with Godwin and Mary-Jane, the nursery quarrels get expressed in a more violent and destructive way in adult life. Claire's seduction of Shelley had all the hallmarks of a quarrel that began in the nursery. 'I want him and you can't have him,' as though Shelley was a toy she was not prepared to share, a conflict that probably began with Claire's battle to gain her stepfather's attention, which she never succeeded in doing. But the nursery quarrel grew and as the children reached adulthood the conflict became dangerously incandescent, fuelled by a belief that the social constraints of consanguinity did not apply. Claire was no relation of Mary, and so she came to believe she had as much right to desire Shelley as had Mary. At such a moment, one of the fundamental structures of our Western family life, centring on kinship ties that are socially arranged around certain rules of incest, such as brothers and sisters not having a sexual relationship, broke down under the strain of sibling rivalry and parental neglect.

I am not claiming that incestuous desire and murderous hatred do not accompany sibling emotions, but for the most part such passions are held in check as family life matures and parents learn how to manage their children's emotions.[28] The moral constraints between unrelated stepsiblings are more complicated because they do not see themselves as blood relations. As already mentioned, the *ménage à trois* of Mary, Shelley and Claire was popularly known as 'The League of Incest' and far from this being, as Shelley dreamed it could be, a more truthful way of accommodating sexual passions, the tortured relationship of the stepsisters never settled into accepted rules that both of them could count upon or trust. In the end, as in the Cinderella tale, the 'ugly sisters,' Fanny and Claire, were the ones who suffered the most from the envious jealousy amongst the stepsiblings. They were the ones, symbolically, whose feet were mutilated and their eyes plucked out.

I have so far traced the vicissitudes of a tragic and entangled family with a complex father and an intemperate stepmother and unhappy and quarrelling stepchildren. I have also spelt out the associations that this live family drama had with our well-known Cinderella fairy story. I now want to end this chapter with a *coda*. A coda, as defined in the *Shorter Oxford Dictionary*, is 'A passage added after the natural completion of a movement so as to form a more definite and satisfactory ending.' It is not so much that this coda makes a 'more definite and satisfactory ending' but this coda brings back a link to the first two chapters in this book. In those chapters there had been a suggestion that underneath or perhaps more accurately lying alongside the well-known Cinderella fairy story lay the story of Donkey-Skin, a tale about a father's lust for his motherless daughter. These two tales were the opposite sides of the same coin and if seen together as a whole, they reveal a profound understanding of the complexity of family life that can follow on from the death of a mother.

The coda I want to add is the discovery that in 1819 Mary Shelley had written a novel called *Mathilda* that was on the theme of father and daughter incest. It was a melodramatic description of the incestuous love between a father and his daughter that had all the hallmarks of a modern day Donkey-Skin. The difference was that *Mathilda* was not a fairy story; it was a story that was wrought from the depths of despair and disillusionment of the author. It was written at a time when Mary Shelley had just lost both her living children and she was full of angry despair that Shelley was in large part to blame for their deaths. But the question is, why did Mary choose to write such a tale? Or put another way, what were the connections between this tale of incestuous desire, Mary's acute depression at the death of her children and her earlier life as a stepchild?

Mary Shelley's relationship with her own children was complicated by echoes of death; her first baby had died soon after birth, in 1815, eleven months later she had a son William born in 1816 and this was followed eighteen months later by the birth of Clara in 1817. Both children, born in England, were healthy and breastfed. But while both Mary's children were well and healthy, Mary could not wholeheartedly rejoice in their well-being because at the time of Clara's birth, Shelley's wife Harriet, whom he had left when he eloped with Mary, drowned herself. Harriet left a motherless son and daughter and throughout the rest of Mary's life, Mary felt guilty about her own part in the death of the mother she had usurped when she eloped with Shelley. And of course, prior to Harriet's death, there had been a more long-lasting guilt that Mary had felt about the death of her mother, Mary Wollstonecraft, whom she came to feel she had killed.

The death of Mary's two children from fever followed within six months of each other in 1818 and 1819 and follows a complicated story, the details of which it is not necessary to go into. Suffice it to say that Mary and Shelley, along with Claire and Allegra, were all living in Italy, at the time, having decided that they would never return to England. Clara was the first child to die of a fever that she caught in the August heat of Tuscany. William's death followed in Rome the next year, and again of fever. But it is worth noting that some of Mary's anger with Shelley that followed on the death of her children, was associated in her mind to his relationship with Claire and her daughter Allegra, who was still alive at this time. Mary was later able to reflect that she had never been able to stand up to either Claire or Shelley because she feared she would be left on her own and had therefore not been able to protect her children well enough. This is a brief account of the background to the agonized mental state Mary was in when she began to write *Mathilda*, in 1819.[29]

It is now necessary to go back and reconsider Mary's relationship with her father Godwin as he enters centre stage and has a very visible presence in the story of *Mathilda* that she was beginning to write. We know that Mary began to have a troubled relationship with her father when Mary-Jane arrived; she not only felt pushed out of the central position she had held in his life, but she felt abandoned when he failed to ever take her side in the rows she had with her stepmother. It has also been suggested, by Holmes, that as Mary's adolescence approached father and daughter had a very entangled relationship that was too close and led to many rows.[30] Mary's anger with Godwin was then augmented when she eloped with Shelley and Godwin refused to see her again or have anything more to do with her until she married Shelley in 1818, following the death of Shelley's wife. Even then Godwin only grudgingly accepted her, though this was a man whose radical philosophy had questioned the need for marriage in his *Political Justice*. Godwin's gradual and half-hearted acceptance of Mary's and Shelley's relationship was more like that of a jealous lover, and here was the centre of Mary's anger towards him as she lashed out at him in her Gothic novel *Mathilda*. One ironical footnote to this novel was that Mary's conscious intention was to earn some money from this novel to help Godwin from his ever increasing and importuning debts that he visited upon her.[31]

Throughout the novel *Mathilda* there are some interesting parallels with Mary's own life. Mathilda's mother dies at her birth, as had Mary's mother. The age of sixteen is also significant in both the novel and in Mary's life. Mathilda's father had abandoned her at birth but returns when she is sixteen. When Mary was sixteen she returned home after eighteen months in Scotland and almost immediately eloped with Shelley. It seems reasonable to imagine that on her return home Mary found herself unreconciled to either her father or her stepmother and her resolution was to run away with Shelley, who had become her father's admiring friend while she had been away. If those are the obvious similarities between Mathilda and her creator Mary, the novel now gives full imaginative vent to Mary's anger and distress.

At the heart of the novel is the seductive betrayal of a tender-hearted daughter by her father. When Mathilda and her father meet for the first time after sixteen years they fall in love with each other and cannot bear to be apart for a moment. This mutual but unconsummated idyll comes crashing down when Mathilda is courted by a young man and her father icily withdraws from her. Mathilda is extremely distressed at her father's unexplained withdrawal from her but as she tearfully implores him to tell her what is in his heart, he gets down on his knee admitting that his withdrawal is because he desires her.

> I . . . had no uneasiness . . . [no] sense of guilt. I loved you as a father might be supposed to love a daughter. . . . But then I saw you become the object of another's love . . . then the fiend awoke in me . . . I . . . imagine[d] that I could conquer my love for you; I never can.[32]

This is the subtle and sadistic twist at the heart of the novel. The novelist Mary, in her imagination, is no longer powerless in the hands of her stepmother and helpless in the entangled relationship of a father who fails to protect her, but in its stead she is redirecting the course of her present anguish. The message of *Mathilda* is that she has a jealous father who cannot bear to witness his daughter's attractiveness to other men, and it does not stretch the imagination too far to believe that this was the message Mary wanted her father, Godwin, to receive. *Mathilda* ends in tragedy; the father drowns himself and Mathilda catches a cold from which she never recovers, even though a Shelley-like figure appears and tries to warm her heart. And one can see that for Mary as she wrote *Mathilda* she felt psychically dead. Her father had failed to recognize his cruel hold upon her, Shelley had failed to protect her, and she was left childless. However the difference between herself and her heroine Mathilda was that she was pregnant with her fourth child, Percy, who did survive and inherit the Shelley title, and this had given her a will to live.

Though there is a sadistic triumph in the novel as Mathilda draws out the confession from her father, it is also a punishing novel and by that I mean there is a constant theme of self-flagellation throughout the book. Mathilda weeps endlessly, first because she is lonely and then because she feels guilty, and this reflects a sense that Mary Shelley is exploring her own state of mind in parallel with Mathilda. We know that Mary, from the moment of birth when her mother died, had been left with a feeling that she had brought about her mother's death, and we see parallels in Mary's description of Mathilda's state of mind. Both heroine and novelist are overburdened with a sorrow that they feel they have brought upon themselves and this leads back to their common experience of both being orphaned at birth, and it is this fact that lies at the heart of the novel and in the tragedy of Mary Shelley's life.

And so in conclusion, my reason for trying to imagine Mary Shelley's state of mind, as her idealized world with Shelley crashed around her following the deaths of her two children, is that Mary Shelley's novella *Mathilda* has echoes of the fairy story of Donkey-Skin and that it offers further insights into family life that follow upon the death of the mother. Both the novel *Mathilda* and Donkey-Skin reach into 'the paradox of incestuous desire,' that is to say, both stories confront the nature of incestuous desire; is it natural or is it the consequence of misfortune such as maternal death or the absence of the mother? Mary Shelley is never explicit about Mathilda's feelings about her father, but Mathilda is certainly emotionally stirred by his revelation of his desire for her, so that when Mathilda's father drowns himself Mathilda comforts herself with fantasies that she will become her father's eternal bride in death. And what is also interesting about that fantasy is that it is a triumph over the dead mother in the novel, and in Mary Shelley's case, it is the triumph over the hated intrusion of her stepmother Mary-Jane Clairmont.

But there is one more thing that can be said about this Gothic novel: Mary Shelley offers a powerful critique of male desire, and its danger, while also attacking the Romantic belief that nature was sublime and could feed the human heart.

The paradox that lies at the heart of this novel is that Mary is suggesting that only in the warmth of human love can the heart grow and flourish, but what happens if this love turns out to be treacherous and dangerous paternal lust? All around her the important men in her life were writing about incestuous desire; Godwin had written about it in his novel *Mandeville*, as had Byron in his poem *Manfred*, and Shelley in his poem *Queen Mab*, and Mary's reply to them, in her novel *Mathilda*, was that such a metaphor has deathly consequences. Mary understood, as these men had not, that if there has been a failure of maternal warmth and love, caused by maternal death, then motherless children would be drawn to paternal warmth like a moth to a flame and this could fan paternal lust.

Mary sent *Mathilda* to Godwin to get it published but Godwin's response to this novel was that it was 'detestable' and 'unpublishable' and he never returned it to Mary.[33] In fact the novel was not published until 1959 when a researcher discovered it among Mary's unpublished papers. And so again we see how difficult it has been culturally for women to offer a critique of male authority and unruly male desire; not least because men have found it 'detestable' to be criticized or to reflect on their behaviour.

It is remarkable that, in following the life of Mary Shelley, many of Godwin's friends likened his wife Mary-Jane Clairmont to the wicked stepmother in Cinderella. When later Mary Shelley wrote her novella *Mathilda* about father and daughter incest, at a moment of extreme loneliness and despair, she seemed to be linking in an uncanny way the Cinderella tale to the other Cinderella tale, Donkey-Skin. In this way Mary Shelley's imaginative life seems to confirm the truth that the Cinderella fairy story and Donkey-Skin are different sides of the same coin. Both of these tales are describing the devastating effect that the death of a mother can have upon the family she leaves behind; all sorts of 'detestable' events can occur.

Notes

1 There was also a stepbrother named Charles Clairmont (1795–1850); see note 10.
2 '*Political Justice & The Vindication of the Rights of Woman* stand together on the shelf like a colossal Pharaoh and his consort, an enduring monument of the spirit of the age' (St Clair 1989 p. 142).
3 Gordon (2015) p. 494.
4 Gordon (2015) p. 20.
5 'Godwin . . . extended his utmost care to the task of education . . . His strictness was undeviating . . . He was too minute in his censures, too grave and severe in his instructions' (Gordon 2015 p. 50). Also Godwin was 'an extreme anarchist idealist, who had been trained for the Presbyterian ministry . . . and always retained the passionate puritan logic of the dedicated religious missionary' (Holmes 1974 p. 98).
6 St Clair (1989) p. 238.
7 See Gordon (2015). Mary Shelley was likened to Cinderella.
8 Holmes (1974) p. 170. See also on Mary-Jane's need to lie, 'no word was ever recorded about the mysterious Mr Clairmont' (St Clair 1989 p. 247). It is worth noting that there has been no biography of Mary-Jane Clairmont. She claimed she had been born in England

and was of noble Huguenot birth but there is no record of her birth. She is supposed to have been born in either 1766 or 1768. There are records that suggest her father may have been a French man, Peter de Vial, living in Exeter, though when she came to sign her marriage certificate to Godwin and to register the birth of her son William Godwin in 1803, she put on both certificates that her father had been Peter Andrew Devereux. When it comes to her mother she may have been a Catherine Oak, or a Mary Tremlett married to a Peter de Vial. But whoever her mother was, the evidence is that she was born before either of Peter de Vial's marriages; see google.com/site/mary-janegodwin. Gordon (2015), Holmes (1974), St. Clair (1989) and Sunstein (1989).

9   Gordon (2015) pp. 21–26.
10 Charles Clairmont did not escape his mother's violent behaviour and was frequently hit. He was sent to Charterhouse School, and then went to Edinburgh to learn about the book trade. He was thankful to leave his difficult home life and as a young man went to Vienna where he taught English and married a Viennese woman and never returned to live in England (St Clair 1989). See also Sunstein (1989).
11 Gordon (2015) p. 215.
12 St Clair (1989) p. 245.
13 'The Clairmonts resented Godwinian condescension; the Godwins despised Clairmont histrionics' (Gordon 2015 p. 215).
14 St Clair (1989).
15 Sunstein (1989).
16 Godwin wrote about a dozen children's books using two pseudonyms, Theophilus Marchcliffe and Edward Baldwin (St Clair 1989 p. 285).
17 The complex character of Godwin is well described by St Clair (1989). Godwin had been sent away from home for two years to a wet nurse. When he returned home he felt disconnected to his parents, whom he despised for having sent him to be 'suckled by a hireling' (p. 1). His strict evangelical upbringing served to reinforce his lifelong difficulty in recognizing his emotions. His inability to integrate his emotions with his rational mind is exemplified by his refusal to have anything more to do with his beloved daughter when she ran off with Shelley. It was only when she was able to marry Shelley, following the suicide of his wife Harriet, that Godwin was prepared to meet her and talk with her, a strange reversal from his earlier philosophical position about marriage as expressed in *Political Justice*.
18 Sunstein (1989) pp. 35–36.
19 In a letter to Byron, Jane, by then calling herself 'Claire,' wrote 'Whatever my feelings of private envy . . . If she were my mortal enemy . . . I would serve her with fidelity and fervently' (Sunstein 1989 p. 142). There is recent documentary evidence that Jane was the illegitimate daughter of Sir William Lethbridge of Taunton. Whether her mother ever told her this is not clear. Google.com/site/maryjane'sdaughter/home/claire'sfather
20 Sunstein (1989).
21 Godwin believed that Allegra was Shelley's child (Sunstein 1989 pp. 173–174).
22 See Holmes (1974), Appendix to Chapter 18, in which he suggests that during this time Shelley was managing the birth of his illegitimate daughter Elena, who was the child of his children's nurse, Elise, and at the same time Claire was having a miscarriage with his child (pp. 481–508). Holmes (1986) later amended this and suggested Elena was in fact adopted (pp. 170–173).
23 See Holmes (1986). In her journal in 1822 Claire wrote, 'I remembered how hopelessly I had lingered on Italian soil for five years, waiting ever for a favourable change, instead of which I was now leaving it having [lost every object – *deleted*] buried there every thing that I loved' (p. 155).
24 See Gordon (2015), who quotes from a letter Mary wrote to Shelley during this time in the late summer of 1815, when she had not seen Shelley for several months. 'Pray is

Clary with you? . . . it would not in the least surprise me if you have written to her from London & let her know that you are there without me that she have taken some such freak –' p. 287. See also Sunstein (1989).
25 Sunstein (1989) p. 332.
26 Sunstein (1989) p. 189.
27 Spark (1987) p. 11.
28 Coles (2003).
29 Sunstein (1989) wrote that this tale, *Mathilda*, was 'one of the first case histories of acute depression, the more rare for being written by the patient' (p. 171). This was echoed by Clemit (2003): 'an uncontrolled expression of Mary Shelley's psychological anxieties' (p. 47 quoted in Shelley (2013)); whereas DiClemidi (2013) suggested Mary Shelley is a more subtle and controlled writer who 'throughout her literary career' explored 'the paradoxes of incestuous desire' (quoted in Shelley 2013 p. xii).
30 See Holmes (1974): 'In many ways the relationship became too close during Mary's adolescence' (p. 170).
31 This was Godwin's letter to Mary, following the death of her son William. He first of all importuned her to send him some money and then he wrote, 'Though at first your nearest connections may pity you in this state, yet . . . when they see you fixed in selfishness and ill humour, and regardless of the happiness of everyone else, they will finally cease to love you, and scarcely learn to endure you' (Gordon 2015 pp. 306–307).
32 Shelley (2013) p. 34.
33 Sunstein (1989).

References

Clemit, P. (2003) *Frankenstein, Mathilda*, and the legacies of Godwin and Wollstonecraft. In *The Cambridge Companion to Mary Shelley*. Ed. E. Schor. Cambridge: Cambridge University Press.

Coles, P. (2003) *The Importance of Sibling Relationships in Psychoanalysis*. London: Karnac Books.

Coles, P. (2015) *The Shadow of the Second Mother: Nurses and Nannies in theories of infant development*. Abingdon: Routledge.

Gordon, C. (2015) *Romantic Outlaws: The Extraordinary Lives of Mary Woolstonecraft and Mary Shelley*. London: Hutchinson.

Holmes, R. (1974) *Shelley: The Pursuit*. London: Elisabeth Sifton Books/Penguin Books.

Holmes, R. (1986) *Footsteps: Adventures of a Romantic Biographer*. London: Flamingo/HarperCollins Publishers.

St Clair, W. (1989) *The Godwins and the Shelleys*. London/Boston: Faber & Faber.

Shelley, M. (2013) *Mathilda and Other Stories*. Introduction and Notes J. DiPlacid. Ware: Wordsworth Classics.

Spark, M. (1987) *Mary Shelley*. Manchester: Carcanet Press Ltd.

Sunstein, E.W. (1989) *Mary Shelley. Romance and Reality*. Baltimore: Johns Hopkins University Press.

Chapter 6

Psychoanalytic theory and stepparents

What does it feel like to be seen as a stepparent while working with a client, as opposed to being seen as a mother or father or sibling or nanny? Who does a stepparent represent in the internal world? These are the questions that a psychological inquiry needs to try and address. One researcher wrote, as if in answer to that question, that the stepparent relationship with a stepchild had 'no moorings in the psyche of the adult' in contrast to one that a stepparent might have with their own child.[1] It may be because of this dislocation or lack of moorings when it comes to thinking about stepparents and stepchildren that we have shown such little interest about them either in clinical work or within our theories. We are literally 'at sea' when it comes to characterizing the nature and effect of the quasi-parental relationships that are created when families divorce and re-marry. This is surprising in the face of widespread divorce. In a report in 2010 one in three marriages ended in divorce in the US and 42 per cent of all marriages in the UK broke up.[2]

In my analytic training stepparenting was never a topic for discussion. This lack of interest in the seismic change that has been taking place within families, over the last forty years, whether in the US or the UK, is surprising. Yet if one picks up any of the current professional journals on therapy today what is constantly reiterated is that there are 'few papers addressing a stepparent, or a step child, or stepgrandparent.'[3] This dearth of clinical material about broken families and stepparents seems to reinforce a belief that they are not important.[4] It also helps to confirm the belief that the most influential aspects of a person's emotional development begin in the earliest months or years of life within an intact family. I had raised the question in my book, *The Shadow of the Second Mother*, as to whether an infant's emotional loyalty might be split if its earliest attachment was to a wet nurse or nanny rather than its mother.[5] But that idea did not address the stepmother or stepfather, who usually enters the family a little later, nor does it address the nature of the stepparent attachment.

A comment by Margaret Robinson (1991), who wrote about the transformation that takes place within a family when there is a divorce, suggests that we all have a basic prejudice against stepparents because we hold to an idealized dream of the nuclear family. This idea may be one important clue as to why there has been such a general lack of clinical work on stepfamilies.[6] But there is another difficulty that confronts stepfamilies. When finally the divorce laws liberated couples, and women in particular, from the chains of a failed marriage, it was an important moment for women's liberation and human rights based upon the concept of equality. Surely, as J.S. Mill (1866) had so passionately argued in his *The Subjection of Women*, this would herald greater human happiness.[7] But has that happened? Are we all happier? Have our divorce laws liberated us? And this is where I come up against an irreconcilable conflict in human rights. There is no longer a moral obligation to endure a cruel and dehumanizing marriage; we have a human right to be treated well. But from the point of view of a child, are we respecting its human rights? All the research evidence is that the child's rights are infringed by divorce. They are seldom thought about or consulted in the heat of divorce, and if they were they would say, however disharmonious the family was, that their deepest wish was for the family to stay together. This was brought home most poignantly in a novel by Elizabeth Strout (2016), in which the narrator of the novel divorces and remarries and so does her husband, but her children rage. Several years later one of the daughters says to the narrator, 'I love him [her stepfather] . . . but I hope he dies in his sleep and then my stepmum can die too, and you and Dad will get back together.'[8] Divorce can liberate adults but it can inflict a wound upon a child's trust that can be damaged for life.

I can see no way around this. I would not want us to go back and impose a demand upon parents to stay together if there are children involved, but equally I want to say, think about your children before you decide to divorce; they have human rights as well. I wonder whether the absence of clinical interest in stepfamilies tells us that we may have turned a blind eye to this human conflict. As Robinson suggested, we hold dear the wish that all families should stay securely attached to each other and we do not want to think about the effect that broken marriages and stepparents are having upon the next generation. We continue to analyse psychic conflict against the Freudian template of the mother and father and child within an intact family. In so doing we forget that even Freudian theory reflects the beliefs about the family of the late nineteenth century and early twentieth century, when the majority of marriages endured, however unhappily. Freud's early case histories, such as Little Hans, Dora and the Wolfman, all came from families where the parents were together.[9] This must have affected his theory about infantile sexual fantasies, for these children's difficulties were always measured against the backdrop of the parents as a married couple.

Freud's ideas have profoundly influenced our understanding of the child's mind, and made us all more aware of its emotional needs, but it is a model that has not considered stepparents and has excluded other important care-taking figures such as wet nurses and nannies, who have played a much larger part in child rearing across all classes than Freud recognized.[10] Freud dealt with these other significant figures in a child's early life by subsuming them under the image of the mother: 'The child's first choice of an object, which derives from its need for help, claims our further interest. Its choice is directed in the first instance to all those who look after it, but these soon give place to its parents.'[11] And one result has been that we have lost sight of these other figures who can jostle for a recognized place in the inner world of the child beside the parents. I often think of the Freudian psychoanalytic model of the family as a Leonardo painting of the Virgin and Child, whereas we may need to be open to the possibility that the inner world is more like a Bruegel village scene.

Once these other significant figures are recognized, a more complex and textured picture of the inner world can be imagined, and fantasies other than those that are solely concentrated upon the parental couple can begin to emerge.[12] We may discover that the stepmother does have some 'psychic moorings' within the internal world; she may be associated with other figures such as a sibling, who was experienced as a rude intrusion, or a dominating aunt who interfered, or a nanny who left unexpectedly. Rather than dismissing the stepmother as representing the split-off feelings of hostility towards the mother, she may begin to take her own place within the family, in all her complexity.

A colleague shared with me that she had patients who had had stepparents but she had never considered that they might enter the therapy in a significant way. She cited a case of a successful businessman whom she saw many years ago in five times a week therapy. A strong therapeutic alliance appeared to have been established and the therapy seemed to go well enough for the first three years and he said he found it helpful. In the fourth year they hit an intense negative phase and he would say 'I hate coming to these sessions!' or 'There is something not right about the room' or 'This is an impossible time for me!' On several occasions he walked out. They both struggled to understand what had provoked this negative therapeutic reaction; the patient himself wondered at the change, but seemed disconnected from his earlier appreciation of the work. What was it that he so disliked about coming to his sessions? The impasse continued and he broke off the therapy.

I learned from my colleague about this man's early life. His mother had been a very difficult woman who was frequently unavailable to him and this had been the main focus of the therapeutic work on his negative feelings towards his therapist. When he was four his parents had divorced and he stayed with his difficult mother and would visit his father at weekends and some holidays. The father remarried almost immediately and these visits became unbearable because he hated his stepmother. Although the patient mentioned the stepmother from time to time in his sessions, always disdainfully, she seemed – to both patient and therapist – to be a subsidiary, even peripheral figure in his psychic life. However the trust that was built up over the years was always susceptible to sudden rupture and it would usually take the form of sharp resentment about something the therapist had said in a recent session. It was at these times that my colleague felt in the presence of another figure, and, in her countertransference, of having no bearings in the work, and of the patient as quite unreachable. For the first three years it was nevertheless possible to restore the therapeutic equilibrium and for the work to continue. It was only in the fourth year that the patient's negative therapeutic reaction got the upper hand.

After the treatment had ended my colleague began to consider how much the patient's stepmother might have been in the consulting room. First as a hated figure who fleetingly appeared in the transference and only in the fourth year as a more unreachable presence. The few exchanges about his stepmother that had taken place seemed thin and ineffectual and, quite naturally, my colleague believed that his relationship with his stepmother had been less formative than his relationship with his mother. When he furiously attacked her for the uncomfortable feelings he was having, in the fourth year of therapy, was there an association to his parent's divorce and his father's remarriage when he was four?

It is an interesting question as to whether the therapy ended in the thrall of a negative transference to his stepmother. In that last year of therapy his painful feelings may have revived memories about his stepmother who had always made him feel she did not want him around. His complaints that the time of his therapy was wrong and the room was wrong may have been an expression of his feelings about his stepmother. I am sure that the work on the negative maternal transference was of importance in this therapy, but nevertheless I was left thinking that we need to be aware that other figures can enter a therapy and cause a major disruption if they are not named.[13] Here is an example of the way a stepparent may enter and disrupt a therapy. And it is for this reason that we need not only to be aware they may be around and take on significance from time to time, but we need to remember that they inevitably have a place, positive or negative, in the internal world of their stepchild. As an addendum, it is interesting to reflect upon my colleague's countertransference feeling, that when they did talk about the stepmother, she felt in the presence of another figure who had no bearings in the work. This would match up with Wallerstein and Lewis's (2007) research findings, quoted at the beginning of the chapter, that for a stepparent the stepchild has 'no moorings in the psyche of the adult.'[14]

The absence of stepparents in Freud's work is surprising because Freud's mother was a stepmother to Freud's two elder half-brothers, and there is evidence that this caused conflict within the family and confusion within the mind of Freud as he grew up.[15] But whatever the reason for Freud's lack of interest in stepparents, it had one interesting consequence. When he wrote about Cinderella he was not interested in it as a fairy story about an unhappy girl who had lost her mother and had a wicked stepmother. Cinderella represented for Freud the archetypal Goddess of Death into whose arms we all eventually return. He writes, she is one of 'the three inevitable relations that a man has with a woman – the woman who bears him, the woman who is his mate and the woman who destroys him [Mother Earth].' He then goes on to add, 'But it is in vain that an old man yearns for the love of a woman as he had it first from his mother; the third of the Fates alone, the Silent Goddess of Death will take him into her arms.'[16]

In Freud's account we have moved a long way from the Cinderella of our fairy stories and her difficult relationship with her stepmother. We can delight in Freud's erudition and see more clearly his deeply held belief that man has always tried to deny that death plays a part in life; but if we are tempted to believe that Cinderella is the representative of the Goddess of Death we are ignoring another meaningful aspect of the tale. The tale also describes the power struggles for life that can take place in families that have been fractured by loss. As we have seen, the death of the mother and the abandonment of children were part of the life of the family until the early nineteenth century, as many social historians have shown us.[17] And these social facts are reflected in many of our fairy stories, and not least the two versions of Cinderella, discussed in the previous chapters. Such tales are profound comments upon how to survive the difficulties that families face when a mother dies and inheritance looms as an ugly figure upon the horizon. The Cinderella story conveys the struggle of families as they deal with this bedrock of tragedy and some of its consequences. What makes the tale both so compelling and uncomfortable to read is that it is about the scarce resources of love that are being fought over. Cinderella, on such an account, is hardly a Goddess of Death, but, if she is a goddess at all, she is a Goddess of Life.

Most theoreticians have followed in Freud's footsteps and have not been concerned about the effect of stepfamilies upon the emotional development of the child. One good example of the way stepfamilies have been ignored within psychoanalytic thinking is to return again to Bruno Bettelheim's *The Uses of Enchantment* that I touched upon in Chapter 2. I now want to consider the way in which the stepmother and the father/stepfather do not have a meaningful position in the fairy stories he considers. Instead we have the uncomfortable experience of Bettelheim pressing his psychoanalytic theories into a neo-Freudian shoe that is too tight.

Bettelheim believed that fairy stories were a handbook for children to help them overcome the existential difficulties that they have to face as they come into conflict with their parents and their siblings. It is surprising to discover that Bettelheim believes that fairy stories have been written with this idea in mind, as he is not only widely read in the history of the fairy story, but he also acknowledges that Cinderella probably originated in China, and was a pagan tale about the death of Cinderella's mother. However the historical origins of such a tale are seen as no more than passing footnotes. Bettelheim is more concerned to persuade us that he has discovered the neo-Freudian key that will unlock the door to the true meaning of these tales, namely that these ancient stories reveal the working and development of the child's mind. So, in the case of the Cinderella tale, it teaches the child that the wicked stepmother is not really a stepmother; she is merely the embodiment of an imaginative figure the child conjures up when it is frustrated and angry with its mother. In other words, the stepmother is only, in the child's mind, a split-off bad mother.

The idea that the stepmother is no more than the imaginary representative of the bad mother in the child's mind may be a way of interpreting the fairy story to a child who does not have a stepmother. And it may be helpful for us all to recognize our capacity to split good from bad, and recognize the way in which we can be critical of those who have occasioned our anger. But Bettelheim's interpretation ignores the stepmother as a real person in the life of many of the early story-tellers and their families and it offers no understanding for children today who may have both a mother and a stepmother. The stepmother needs to be incorporated into our understanding of the meaning of such tales. Furthermore it is not an adequate understanding of the impact of the trauma of divorce, or death of the mother, to posit that 'What goes on in reality is less important than what goes on in our mind.'[18] Not least because, in this case, it leads to the dismissal of the child's experience of a real stepmother. In Bettelheim's hands she becomes no more than the symbolic representation of the 'bad' aspects of the real mother, whom the child is struggling to integrate with the 'good' mother, who is much loved. And so in Bettelheim's hands the wheel turns back on itself and we can see more clearly why the stepmother is of little interest to the psychoanalytic model of the mind.

I have already discussed in Chapter 2 the way Bettelheim treats the Wolf in *Little Red Riding Hood* as no more than the grandmother in disguise, in other words children need not be frightened of what strange men might do to them. He does something slightly different when it comes to fathers/stepfathers in our fairy stories. He treats them as a rare species especially when it comes to that difficult Cinderella fairy story of *Donkey-Skin*, in which the father has incestuous desires for his daughter. He recognizes that 'Cinderella flees from a father who wants to marry her.' But how does he understand a father who desires his daughter? Not as one might have hoped, with some acknowledgement of paternal responsibilities. On the contrary, this 'oedipal entanglement of father and daughter' in which the father 'should want her [Cinderella] to love him beyond reason,' is no more than 'a projection of a little girl's wish.'[19] So parental desire is no more than the Oedipal fantasies of the child. Again, as with the stepmother, we are left with the proposition that 'it is all in the mind' and not the mind of the father but in the mind of the child.

At the very least Bettelheim's psychoanalytic account of the fairy story, and in particular Cinderella, is narrowed by his neo-Freudian interpretation and is not a rich enough description of the many layers to this tale. As one critique observed, 'He treats [fairy stories] so to speak, as flattened out, like patients on a couch, in a timeless contemporaneity.'[20] We can appreciate that Bettelheim is giving an account of the psychological capacity of the human mind to split between love and hate and he hopes to show the way hate can be projected outward onto people who can be safely disparaged in this way; but to say that the stepmother is no more than a projection of the child's anger with the mother, and that the father's incestuous desire only reflects the child's infantile Oedipal wishes, is a travesty of a more thoughtful appreciation of the real difficulties that stepfamilies face. We have already seen that the traducing of oral tales into children's fairy stories began to take place in the eighteenth and nineteenth century, and now it needs to be added there has been a twentieth-century post-Freudian interpretation of these fairy stories, such as Bettelheim's interpretation, that reflects a further traducing of them. Fairy stories seem to be particularly vulnerable to interpretations that reveal more about the writer's social attitudes and beliefs about children and the bourgeois family rather than the ever shifting struggle of man to give meaning to his fate.

Our psychoanalytic thinking has not kept up with the social and cultural changes that have been taking place within the family, in which at least one third of the children born in this country will have known the break-up of the original family.[21] The idea that marriage lasted a lifetime has vanished and yet there is almost no discussion about whether our classical Freudian model of mental health, that postulates a mother and father and child, can assimilate the new forms of relationships that are taking place. Furthermore, as we shall see in the next chapter, we have to turn to research and self-help books if we want to understand the emotional effect upon our children of the new patterns of child rearing in which many find themselves with stepparents.[22]

It is hard at times not to think that there is a silent refusal within the therapy world to take on board that the family structure is changing. One gets the impression that the new forms of family life, wherein many children will have experienced their family breaking up, is being ignored. It is as though Rome is burning and we are unable to think of the suffering that it is causing. I find this surprising because over the last forty years there has been a significant shift within psychoanalytic thinking about the nature of man. There has been increasing discomfort with the idea of man as a lonely figure battling against his future, such as depicted by the eighteenth-century republican painter Frederich David (1774–1840). Many of David's paintings show a bleak landscape in which a solitary figure looks out onto the world. There have been important figures within the psychoanalytic world, such as Bowlby (1969) and Rutter (1991) who have suggested that our psychological survival depends upon our relationships to others. In other words, man is relationship seeking.[23] This idea has been corroborated by the research into the neuroscience of the brain, led by such theoreticians such as Panksepp (1998), Schore (2002), and McGilchrist (2009). They are all suggesting that the biological substrate of our emotions requires fine attunement from our caregivers if we are to flourish psychologically. These ideas do suggest that we have the tools to furnish an important conceptual shift in the way we think about psychic reality. We can imagine the complexity of the way we weave our experiences with others alongside our imagination, so that inner fantasy and outer reality are in a more complex dialogue.

A question does still arise with attachment theory about stepparents. If, as most theoreticians agree, the earliest relationship of the infant at the breast of the mother is where our secure or insecure attachments begin, then it does mean that the stepmother must necessarily play a secondary role in the understanding of the foundation blocks of mental health or distress. In the case of the infant who forms an insecure attachment to the mother, can a stepmother form a secure attachment to her stepchild later? Can she replace the mother in this way? Or is the stepmother and stepchild relationship always undermined by the earlier insecure attachment? How do we let her in to the building of earlier psychic structures? Attachment theory has brought about a significant change in the way we think about man's needs for relationships. But the role that stepparents play in the psychic development of the child still needs further exploration.

To return to my earlier point about an irreconcilable conflict between the needs of adults and the needs of children, we know that children of divorced parents are bewildered, angry, confused and some can be left with a long-lasting fear that relationships cannot be depended upon. The adults, however unfortunate their marriage may have been, suffer also. This is not to say all families with children should stay together, however unhappy and dysfunctional the family may be; but it is to say that the research that has been done on the consequences of divorce, whatever the viewpoint of the researchers, shows that divorce causes suffering all round. This is the fact of the matter and we need to find ways of recognizing this suffering and ameliorating it. I have posited a further difficulty: can we be sure that a good early relationship at the breast is enough to shield the child from a later psychic earthquake?

I recently read a paper that did mention divorce and stepparents and I was delighted because it is one of the few clinical accounts I have been able to find.[24] However I found myself disappointed by the end, because the stepparents were only mentioned and were never given a part to play in the analysis. In the way I describe this paper I could be accused of traducing the text, which is in a way true, but it seems to me it offers an example of current clinical work that ignores the presence of stepparents. It is in many ways a very sensitive and painful account of a three times a week therapy with a young woman. Her difficulty was that she felt empty and spent her fantasy life dreaming about meeting a Prince Charming. When she thought she had met him she always ended up disappointed by him and enraged. There is a brief account of this woman's early life. Her parents had met while studying at university and married. They divorced when she was two. Her father moved abroad and remarried and thereafter this young woman had to fly on her own to see her father and stepmother, to comply with the custodial arrangements. Some time later her mother remarried and she went with her mother and stepfather to live abroad.

The trauma, if that is the right word, that hit both patient and analyst was that in the third year of therapy this young woman developed leukaemia. And the rest of the therapy was about how both analyst and client came to understand the psychological meaning of her illness. The analyst gives a very thoughtful account of the 'black hole' that had been left in this woman's mind as her parents' marriage disintegrated. His understanding of this woman's mental state included the intergenerational difficulties that her very young and narcissistic parents were facing as a consequence of their early experiences. He called her leukaemia an embolism, or obstruction, that came between them, patient and analyst, that was similar to her parents' failure to empathise with her even before she was born, but the principal failure was the mother's to nurture her infant.

In many ways it is a convincing explanation of the way a memory of pre-verbal trauma can announce itself or find a way of expressing itself. But I was left wondering whether there were other factors that had contributed to her 'blockage.' In the first place I was quite struck that this young woman's leukaemia occurred in the third year of analysis. We are not told what was happening to her when she was three, but we do know that her parent's marriage broke up when she was two and she had to fly abroad on her own to visit her father and stepmother from an early age. I suspect she may have been about three when this travelling trauma was inflicted on her. Wallerstein and Lewis's (2007) research on the effect of divorce on young children found that very young children who were sent on their own on long and unfamiliar journeys to one of their parents were severely traumatized; this was the most extreme experience of disintegration to which they could be subjected. They could feel they were literally flying apart. If on top of that terror they then had to adjust to an estranged father and a strange and unfamiliar stepparent, the stepparent could become associated with the feeling they were falling into a 'black hole.'

So what I am saying is, I can imagine that if a client who comes to us from a broken home and expresses the fear of falling into a 'black hole,' I would expect to find other contributory factors to this annihilation anxiety than that associated with her parents' separation and her mother's lack of empathy. The anxiety may have been perpetrated by the parents' past difficulties and their difficulty in nurturing their child. But I would want to go on and suggest that the break-up of the marriage may have a forward trajectory that affects the child as well. By that I mean I could imagine that the young woman was trying to metabolise and express the terror of what then happened to her. Something unimaginably terrifying happened to her when she was left to fly off alone to somewhere with no one alongside her. So a question might be, was she feeling at that moment in the third year of therapy that she was a three-year-old flying somewhere unknown where she would meet an estranged father and an unwelcomed stepmother? Surely the black hole contained a non-containing mother, an estranged father, an unwelcoming stepmother and later a stepfather, and if that is so, their separate roles need to be distinguished.

As I end this chapter I want to reflect on the difficulty I have had in writing it. I cannot find clinical material that might help in understanding the place that stepparents surely play in the unfolding development of a stepchild. Of course it could be the case that therapists do not believe that stepparents have any significant role in the inner world of the child, which is the impression I get from the clinical case I have just cited. But I am putting such an idea aside. I want to suggest that there are therapies, as cited at the beginning of this chapter, that can founder on an unrecognized stepparent transference. The problem is that they have not yet been written about. Yet surely it must be there? There was a nice moment in Grayson Perry's (2016) book *The Descent of Man* when he was attending a group therapy. He could not understand why he took an instant and violent dislike to a young man within the group. It was only later, when he was talking with his individual therapist, that Perry realized that his rage against this young man was because he was reminded of his violent stepfather. 'I realized this fellow was the same age and had the same appearance as my stepfather when he moved in.'[25] I think many of us may be walking around projecting earlier feelings we may have had about our stepparents onto unsuspecting people we meet, as was the case with Perry and the young man in his therapy group. I recognize that Perry wrote that he had been helped by his personal therapist to understand some of the reasons for his hatred of this young man. So it is clear that there are therapists who recognize the way stepparents can continue to cause emotional disruption in their stepchildren's life. The only point I am making is that such a stepparent transference has not yet been written about in clinical papers in the UK.

I need to add a postscript. I had finished this chapter when I encountered a therapist with whom I shared my bewilderment that I could find no account of a stepparent transference in the clinical literature. He gave me a paradoxical reply. He told me he had been seen as a hated stepfather in a therapy and for several years his patient had been very angry with him, and presumably, though I failed to ask him, he had acknowledged this role in the therapy, because the therapy moved on and the patient did not walk out. But, he went on to say, when he published the clinical case he had not thought it was significant to write about stepparents. When I asked him why, he said that in time the therapy moved on and the significant work that they had subsequently done had been about the psychic fracture that had taken place in his patient when her parents divorced. He saw his task was to help her to resolve this Oedipal fracture.

He elaborated further about what he meant when he said that one reason for not writing about stepparents in the psychic development of a child of divorce was that the psychoanalytic task is to help the child to an Oedipal resolution. This is difficult if the parents are no longer together and the parental couple is now a mother and stepfather, and father and stepmother. In psychoanalytic terms the 'primal scene' has been distorted, but the task nevertheless is to find a way of bringing the parents back into some sort of Oedipal resolution. He then added a final comment about why psychoanalysis did not need to take into account the role that stepparents might play. Stepparents play the same symbolic function as parents. It is that belief that I am sure explains why psychoanalytic theory has not considered stepparents.

There are two points I want to make about these comments. Of course the psychic fracture that takes place when a child's parents divorce is crucially important, especially if they are very young at the time. But if we are unaware of the part stepparents can play in the evolving psychic structure of their stepchild, we may fail to understand an important transference. The therapist I spoke to weathered this stormy stepfather transference, but I would have liked to hear how he did. He did say that the hostility directed towards him did directly refer to an unkind and violent stepfather and not the father. But surely we as clinicians need to know about such a transference, not least because his patient did not have a father who behaved in this way. Stepparents may not be the central focus of the work, long term, but it is my contention that if we do not know that there can be a stepparent transference, and that it can be distinguished from a parental one, we are contributing to the social and cultural and psychological prejudice against stepparents and their stepchildren, but we are also limiting our understanding of the multifarious nature of the unconscious and 'its manifestations, its contents and its structure.'[26]

Notes

1 Wallerstein and Lewis (2007) p. 457.
2 Wallerstein and Lewis (2007), Leach (2014).
3 Delgado (2003) p. 1063.
4 Psychoanalytic Electronic Publishing Web (P.E.P web). Available at http://psychoanalysis.org.uk/publications/pep-web. There are 766 citings of the word 'stepmother' but not a single article on the problems of being a stepmother.
5 Coles (2015).
6 Robinson (1991).
7 Mill (1866) *The Subjection of Women*.
8 Strout (2016) p. 190. I want to thank Dorothy Judd for suggesting I read this novel.
9 Freud, 'Little Hans' (1909), 'Dora' (1905) and 'The Wolfman' (1918).
10 Coles (2015).
11 Freud (1910) p. 47.
12 See Coles (2003) on the concept of the sibling transference.
13 Coles (2011).
14 'The stepparent relationship with the child has no moorings in the psyche of the adult. The child is not the fruit of the bond that unites the new couple. It is in fact a foreign body' (Wallerstein and Lewis 2007 p. 457).
15 'Gay (1988) is surely right when he suggests that Freud's mind was made up of "childhood conundrums" in which his half-brother was a father, his father was a grandfather to his closest playmate, he . . . was an uncle to his older nephew [and] his mother was the same age as his half-brother' (Coles 2003 p. 38).
16 Freud (1913) pp. 298–312. Freud wrote this paper at the time when the storm clouds of the First World War were gathering, and he was deeply troubled.
17 See in particular Boswell (1988) and Fildes (1988).
18 Bettelheim (1976) p. 258.
19 Bettelheim (1976) pp. 245–246.
20 Darnton (1984) p. 13.
21 Leach (2014), Robinson (1991) and Wallerstein, Lewis and Blakeslee (2002).
22 I am leaving out of my discussion the effects on the emotional development of the child who is brought up by two parents of the same sex.
23 Bateson (1973).
24 Magnenat (2016) p. 41.
25 Perry (2016) p. 130.
26 Jacobs (2017) p. 24.

References

Bateson, G. (1973) *Steps to an Ecology of Mind*. UK: Paladin.
Bettelheim, B. (1976) *The Uses of Enchantment: The Meaning and Importance of Fairy Tales*. London: Penguin Books.
Boswell, J. (1988) *The Kindness of Strangers: The Abandonment of Children in Western Europe from Later Antiquity to the Renaissance*. London: Penguin.
Bowlby, J. (1969) *Attachment and Loss. Vol. 1*. London: Hogarth Press.
Coles, P. (2003) *The Importance of Sibling Relationships in Psychoanalysis*. London/New York: Karnac.
Coles, P. (2011) *The Uninvited Guest from the Unremembered Past*. London: Karnac.
Coles, P. (2015) *The Shadow of the Second Mother: Nurses and Nannies in Theories of Development*. London/New York: Routledge.

Darnton, R. (1984) *The Great Cat Massacre and Other Episodes in French Cultural History.* New York: Basic Books.

Delgado, S. (2003) Stepparenting: Creating and Recreating Families in America Today. *Psychoanalytic Quarterly.* 72: 1052–1057.

Fildes, V. (1988) *Wet Nursing: A History from Antiquity to the Present.* Oxford: Basil Blackwell.

Freud, S. (1905) Fragment of an Analysis of a Case of Hysteria. In *The Standard Edition of the Complete Psychological Works of Sigmund Freud. Vol. VII.* London: Hogarth Press.

Freud, S. (1909) Analysis of a Phobia in a Five-Year-Old Boy. In *The Standard Edition of the Complete Psychological Works of Sigmund Freud. Vol. X.* London: Hogarth Press.

Freud, S. (1910) Five Lectures in Psychoanalysis. In *The Standard Edition of the Complete Psychological Works of Sigmund Freud. Vol. 11.* London: Hogarth Press.

Freud, S. (1913) The Three Caskets. In *The Standard Edition of the Complete Psychological Works of Sigmund Freud. Vol. XII.* London: Hogarth Press.

Freud, S. (1918) From the History of an Infantile Neurosis. In *The Standard Edition of the Complete Psychological Works of Sigmund Freud. Vol. XVII.* London: Hogarth Press.

Jacobs, A. (2017) Rethinking Matricide. In *The Mother in Psychoanalysis and Beyond.* Ed. R. Mayo and C. Moutsou. London/New York: Routledge.

Leach, P. (2014) *Family Breakdown: Helping Children Hang on to Both Parents.* London: Unbound.

Magnenat, L. (2016) Psychosomatic Breast and Alexithymic Breast: A Bionian Psychosomatic Perspective. *International Journal of Psychoanalysis.* 97. 1: 41–63.

McGilchrist, I. (2009) *The Master and the Emissary: The Divided Brain and the Making of the Western World.* New Haven/London: Yale University Press.

Mill, J.S. (2006 [1866]) *On Liberty and the Subjection of Women.* Ed. A. Ryan. London: Penguin Classics.

Panksepp, J. (1998) *Affective Neuroscience: The Foundation of Human and Animal Emotions.* New York: Oxford University Press.

Perry, G. (2016) *The Descent of Man.* London: Allen Lane.

Robinson, M. (1991) *Family Transformation through Divorce and Remarriage: A Systemic Approach.* Abingdon: Routledge.

Rutter, M. (1991) *Maternal Deprivation Reassessed.* 2nd edition. London: Penguin Books.

Schore, A.N. (2002) Advances in Neuropsychoanalysis: Attachment Theory and Trauma Research: Implications for Self-psychology. *Psychoanalytic Inquiry.* 22: 433–484.

Strout, E. (2016) *My Name is Lucy Barton.* New York/London: Penguin Books.

Wallerstein, J. and Resnikoff, D. (1997) Parental Divorce and Developmental Progression: An Inquiry into Their Relationship. *International Journal of Psycho-Analysis.* 78. 1: 135–155.

Wallerstein, J., Lewis, J. and Blakeslee, S. (2002) *The Unexpected Legacy of Divorce. A 25 Year Landmark Study.* London: Fusion Press.

Wallerstein, J. and Lewis, J. (2007) Sibling Outcomes and Disparate Parenting and Stepparenting after Divorce: Report from a 10-Year Longitudinal Study. *Psychoanalytical Psychology.* 24: 445–458.

Wallerstein, J., Lewis, J. and Rosenthal, S.P. (2013) Mothers and Their Children after Divorce. *Psychoanalytical Psychology.* 30. 2: 167–187.

Chapter 7

Is stepparenting all in the mind?

I ended the last chapter with the idea that if we have had stepparents in all probability we project our feelings about them onto other people, from time to time. I cited Perry's (2016) rage against a young man in his therapy group as a case in point. The young man reminded him of his violent stepfather and at that moment his feelings about his suffering under the hands of his stepfather overwhelmed him. He could not see the young man for himself, especially when the young man cracked his finger joints just as his stepfather had many years before. Perry is not alone in having suffered under the hands of a stepparent. Two thousand years ago Euripides may have had a similar feeling when he warned 'Better a serpent than a stepmother'![1] What I have found so striking, as a psychotherapist, is the way in which there has been unwillingness to let the stepmother into the psychoanalytic Garden of Eden, even though she has played a significant and difficult part in family life across the centuries.

When I say that we probably project feelings we had about our stepparents onto other people during the course of our life, what exactly do I mean? In the case of Perry, his father had walked out when he was very little and he did not see him again throughout his childhood. Yet there is a brooding sense in Perry's reminiscences that he needed him and missed him. When his stepfather arrived a few years later, he was not the father that Perry wanted or needed. He was a man in a rage and he had no compunction in being violent and terrifying to Perry as a young boy. So when I talk of Perry's transference to the young man in his therapy group, it must have been a complicated mix of feelings of anger but probably of sadness and loss as well. This young man will have conjured up feelings that went beyond the stepfather into the fractured world of Perry's childhood. The notion that I am pursuing is only to say that if we have stepparents then they will be remembered in all sorts of ways; not least we may have feelings about quite innocent individuals we meet who suddenly call up memories and emotions that are attached to our stepmother or stepfather. This can occur in therapy at moments where the therapist becomes the catalyst for emotions that may have lain hidden. I shall return to these issues in greater detail in the next chapter, when I speculate from the interviews that I have had with people who have known about stepfamilies.

The place I have had to turn to in order to understand about the complex emotions that surround stepparents are autobiographies and self-help books, that come predominantly from the US. One particularly vivid account of being a stepmother was written by a well-known English journalist, Brenda Maddox (1975) in *The Half-Parent*.[2] It is unflinching in its depiction of the 'hell' of being a stepmother. Her reason for writing the book was that she had found there was very little help when she became a stepparent, even though there were and still are an unprecedented number of children who have stepparents. She corroborates the impression that therapists and psychiatrists have been pretending 'there is no such thing' as divorce.[3] Yet, she says, there are those in the real world who do know about such things, and as an example she cites a letter William Gladstone wrote to Margot Asquith, when she married and took on Asquith's five orphaned children: 'It is work far beyond human strength'![4] Maddox provides a thoughtful way in which we might try and elaborate on the problems that accompany stepparenting.

One interesting idea she explored was whether we were witnessing a new or emerging 'form of kinship' taking place in Western society.[5] In one sense it would fit with Wallerstein and Lewis's (2007) point, made some years later, that stepparents have 'no psychic moorings' with their stepchild.[6] This was similar to an image Molly Gibson in Chapter Four used about herself when confronted with a stepmother. In the case of Molly it described the experience a child might have when a stepparent enters the family; the child feels cast adrift from all its safe moorings. If we shift the metaphor to a different angle it may be that stepparents have 'no psychic moorings' because we have not given them the space or time to incorporate them into our concept of the inner world of the unconscious. The challenge is how to delineate some of the complicated emotional effects of this new kinship system so that we do at last give stepparents and stepchildren a 'psychic mooring.'

The idea of a new kinship system has been described in several ways, of which the most quoted has been the idea that we are moving into 'the blended family.'[7] Others have written of 'serial monogamy' or 'progressive polygamy.'[8] Whatever the chosen term might be there has been a recognition that 'the growth of stepfamilies has been one of the most dramatic changes in British and American family life in recent decades.'[9] What has been surprising is that the recognition that new forms of family life are emerging has elicited quite passionate and contradictory responses. For instance, the famous anthropologist, Margaret Mead, who studied different forms of family life in Papua New Guinea, wrote,

> We have constructed a family system which depends upon fidelity, lifelong monogamy, and the survival of both parents. But we have never made adequate social provision for the security and identity if that marriage is broken. ... We have, in fact ... saddled ourselves with a system that won't work.[10]

Others have gone to great lengths to reassure divorcing parents that the hellish tempest will abate and a new happy family can be created. A good example of this latter optimism is in a self-help book, *Stepfamilies: Love, Marriage and Parenting in the First Decade* by James Bray and John Kelly (1999). This is a practical and sensible book based on a nine-year study of 200 families, 100 that are intact and 100 that have divorced. They do not investigate the subtle psychological conflicts about becoming a stepparent, or having a stepparent, but nevertheless they give robust encouragement to those who are suffering the stress of divorce. The overall message is that stepfamilies can succeed and children whose parents have divorced are not scarred for life, providing all the members of the new families can behave reasonably.

One of the salient points that is made is that it takes at least two years for a re-formed family to settle into its new lifestyle, and during that time stepparents are counselled to be patient and temperate and to try to make friends with their stepchildren, rather than to insist they are the new mother or father. The finding of this warm-hearted book is that it challenges 'conventional wisdom [that] has held that divorce permanently scars a child.'[11] Bray and Kelly's message is that if you set out on this journey it is going to be a difficult one; you will find that you will be treated with hostility by your stepchildren; the ghosts of your failed marriage will be waiting to haunt you; you will be tempted to break up this new relationship when it is difficult and finally your self-esteem will be challenged by the biological parents of your stepchildren. But if you are prepared for all this, then there is no reason why your new family should not flourish and no long-lasting psychological damage need be done to your children and stepchildren. No precise numbers are given but we are led to believe that the majority of re-formed families have happy outcomes. It is only a minority who fail and break up and marry again or 'seemed only to survive but not to thrive.'[12]

This is where the work of Judith Wallerstein (2002) and colleagues over the last twenty-five years offers some more challenging thoughts than those of Bray and Kelly. They have provided strenuous psychological appreciation of the emotional effects upon the children of divorce, both in the US and the UK. The original research began in 1971 in California and ended in 1994. It would seem that one of the major concerns behind this research was the fact that 'there has been hardly any exploration of the stepparent's role either as an influence on the biological parent's relationship with his or her children or as a direct influence on the stepchildren.'[13] They limited themselves to research on the relationships between mothers and children after divorce, rather than on re-formed families following divorce. So the criticism of their research might be that it only takes into account one angle of divorce and its effects. But nevertheless their research is detailed and extensive.

The children that were followed over the years of this research were described, pre-divorce, as 'on target' emotionally, socially and intellectually, yet as the stress of divorce and break-up was being felt, one half of the children were 'unhappy, and lagging in the social and academic behaviour.'[14] One important factor that their study revealed was that when parents divorced there was a tendency to treat their children unequally, in other words, they might favour one child and scapegoat the other.[15] If this unequal favouritism occurred, whether it was by the mother or the father, it had a long-lasting and detrimental effect upon the scapegoated child. They also discovered that, as the Cinderella fairy story had already warned us, a stepmother would favour her own children over those of her stepchildren. But nevertheless their figures seem to suggest some similarity with Bray and Kelly's findings. They found that post divorce, nearly half of mothers and children maintained good relationships; just over a quarter of mothers experienced a disrupted relationship with their children for about four years that was gradually restored; and only a quarter of all divorcing families left their children with long-lasting mental health problems. And not surprisingly these were families where the mother had fragile mental health prior to the divorce.

There was a heartbreaking account in the Wallerstein research of scapegoating in the case of a five-year-old girl whose parents had an unresolved and acrimonious divorce. The marriage had fallen apart due to the father's abusive and violent behaviour towards the mother when drunk. He was a good father to his two children, a son of seven and a daughter aged five. But once the divorce took place, the father visited his anger with his wife upon his daughter, while nurturing his son. He would say things to her such as 'you are stupid like your mother' and this type of behaviour continued throughout the girl's childhood visits to her father. Wallerstein's summary of this experience was to say that at the twenty-five year follow-up, this young woman 'had become anxious, timid, self-deprecating . . . [and] allowed her boyfriends to exploit and physically abuse her.'[16] In other words, the father's treatment of his daughter was lastingly destructive to her mental health.

In contrast to the effect that this father had upon his daughter through his unmediated anger towards his wife, in another clinical case there is a description of the amazing resilience of a four-year-old boy whose parents separated. In this case the mother was a promiscuous and a drug addicted young woman, who abandoned her son for about a year, and the father sank into a life threatening depression. In spite of these unpropitious beginnings, this little boy, when he was interviewed at seventeen, had done well both at school and with his peers. He had had five play sessions with a therapist for two years from the age of six, and this therapist treated him with imaginative sympathy and love. It was this therapist who then interviewed him at seventeen and it is clear they were both delighted to see each other again and had a lively memory of their encounter. But we are not led to believe that it was these five therapy sessions that made the difference to this young man's well-being at seventeen. The conclusion that Wallerstein et al. made about this remarkable young man was that his parents had always loved him and never fought over him, and they had never denigrated each other, even though they could not manage a life together. In other words, the pragmatic assumption that Wallerstein et al. are making is that if the parents have the capacity to imagine that they need to support their child's love and loyalty to both parents, then the child has some hope of not being too damaged by their separation.[17]

Perhaps the most challenging observation of this twenty-five year study on divorce was that 'early attachment patterns are subject to change by later life experience' and therefore, the concept of a secure early attachment is not a sure guide to later emotional stability.[18] They quote from a twenty-year longitudinal study on attachment and it was found that a child with a secure attachment to its mother could have that attachment dislodged by subsequent trauma, such as death or divorce.[19] This presents a challenge if the present trend towards increasing numbers of divorcing families continues. There may be more stepmothers and stepfathers bringing up other people's children, and one consequence we can be sure about is that the childhood of these children of divorced parents will no longer be described as 'carefree' or as 'roaming the daisied fields.'[20]

Wallerstein's and her colleagues' research takes us into another important debate about marriage and divorce. The 1948 UN Charter of Human Rights in Article 16 (3) states that 'The Family is the natural and fundamental group unit of society' and yet one in three marriages end in divorce and 'about fifty per cent of children will not grow in what has been known as a "traditional family life"' and 'one in four [will] grow up in a stepfamily.'[21] So are we witnessing something 'unnatural' in our society in the face of so many marriages breaking up? Or is divorce the 'natural' outcome of the immense cultural shifts that have taken place in the US and the UK over the last forty years? Are we having difficulty in recognizing or adapting to changes in gender roles; changes in the way we think about human rights; changes in women's rights, as well as changes about the meaning that is given to a life? And here we see a subtle and complex debate about whether the ubiquity of divorce is creating a generation of people whose 'natural rights' are being corroded. Wallerstein and colleagues make clear that all children suffer when their parents divorce. They live in 'a parallel universe' to children who come from an intact family, even a family with tension and arguments between the parents. And even other researchers, who have a fundamental disagreement with Wallerstein's beliefs, agree that the children of divorce do less well at school.[22] But the belief that children of divorced families suffer leads into a controversy that besets therapeutic intervention. Do these scars last for a lifetime or can favourable life experiences heal these wounds? Or put another way, can a child's secure attachment be undermined by the disruption of family life, as the research quoted above suggests?

Wallerstein's work has been taken to task because it has been said that she brings to her research a deeply held belief that all children suffer when their parents divorce. In the words of Barnes and colleagues (1997), Wallerstein's work 'is seriously misleading as a whole because it is based on a sample of children who came to her clinic precisely because they were suffering and needed help,' and added to that was 'her determination . . . to convey the emotional impact of separation on children' that biased her findings.[23] In fact, Wallerstein states that her research was based on families who had been referred by their attorney to her Center for Families in Transition, and they were specifically chosen because 'they were developmentally on track, never having been referred for emotional or developmental problems.'[24] So we see the battle lines are drawn and emotions run high when the children of divorce are thought about. I do not want to get into the debate between Barnes et al. and Wallerstein et al., and denigrate one research finding against another, but it seems to me that most researchers that I have read would agree with Wallerstein's findings that about a quarter of the children they observed failed to recover from their parents' divorce, and that was due to the fragile state of the mother's mind, even before divorce.[25] Where the chief disagreement lies is that Wallerstein, who is looking at the effect on young people when their parents divorce, believes that 'We have not fully appreciated how divorce continues to shape the lives of young people after they reach *full adulthood.*'[26] Other researchers are more sanguine about the long-term effects of divorce. For instance, Robinson (1991) has an angle of vision that is more anthropological, and nearer the view of stepparenting as creating new kinship ties. She writes that there are major benefits associated with stepparenting, that is to say,

> the burdens of parenting can be shared with the 'other' subsystem of the reformed extended family system. This not only gives both parents and each household some respite, but it also brings greater objectivity into the whole system than is usually possible for the biological parents to achieve.[27]

And Maddox, in her frank and vivid description of the early hellish years of stepparenting, ends reflectively with the observation, 'Stepfamilies can be happy, even happier than families in which there has never been more than one mother and father, but it takes more work.'[28] It is interesting to note that Robinson's and Maddox's books were written from the inside perspective of being stepmothers, whereas Wallerstein states quite clearly that she has known fifty-three years of happy marriage to her well-known psychoanalyst husband Robert Wallerstein. In other words however objective we might wish to be about our views on divorce, it is difficult to get away from the fact that our personal experiences influence our thinking, or as J.S. Mill put it, 'travelling men usually see only what they already had in mind.'[29]

To return to Maddox's challenging idea that divorcing families are creating a new form of kinship system, what might that mean? In the first instance, re-formed families can never be the same as those where the couple stay together over a lifetime. A stepchild may have two mothers and two fathers, and the child will surely be facing a very different psychological task, as it develops and has to negotiate adulthood, in comparison with a child who only has one set of parents. Yet if we persist in being uninterested in these secondary relationships and the impact they have upon the child's emotional development and even in the attachment patterns, then the child will not find adequate psychological help when in difficulty. If we fail to imagine that there could be a transference to a stepparent then, as I suggested in the last chapter, the therapist might find the therapy has come to an abrupt end. The tragedy, if that should happen, is that no one has gained any insight into what was happening and the client may be left with the omnipotent belief that the stepparent has been got rid of, as they triumphantly walk out of therapy.

One woman I interviewed had had a stepmother. Her mother had died when she was quite young and her father had married soon after. When later she went into therapy her therapist concentrated on helping her mourn the loss of her mother. This was of course hugely significant and when she finished her therapy much of her internal grief had been faced. Many years later she went back into therapy with a different analyst, following the death of her lover. In this therapy she discovered a rage within herself that she attributed to her therapist not understanding her. And she soon left. It was only some time later as she began to recover from the loss of her lover that she began to wonder why she had been so angry with this second therapist. It occurred to her that her rage with the therapist was associated to her stepmother. She felt that the very language that her second therapist used was wrong and she felt misunderstood. In fact English was not the first language of either her stepmother or her therapist, and this gave added substance to her feeling that they both spoke 'a foreign language' that ignored her pain and anguish. I think we could say that the rage with her therapist, that led her to walk out of the therapy, was directed towards an unrecognized transference towards the stepmother, who had tried to take her mother's place in her childhood. Would it have made any difference if her first therapist had recognized that in her internal world her client had a mother and a stepmother? Might the client have been less enraged with her second therapist if she had been helped to understand the rage she had felt towards her stepmother? There are of course no answers to those questions, but surely we can say that this woman's feelings about her stepmother had a life of their own and had probably influenced her emotional life without anyone recognizing them.

On the positive side, Robinson's reflections, quoted above, about the possible benefits of what she calls 'a reformed extended family system' or Maddox's 'new kinship system' might help to shift the negative images we do have about stepmothers and stepfathers. It seems unquestionable that stepparents start with a disadvantage. Divorce means that the original marriage has broken up because it has become untenable; the stable walls of family life have fallen down and stepparents can never rebuild the original dwelling, though most children will hope that they can. So the question might be, can the new dwelling that is built on a reformed family system be just as good as the earlier one? And alongside that question is a further one, can stepparents and stepchildren form attachments that will secure future well-being?

One feature of this 'new kinship system' is that it is built upon the foundation stones of loss, discord and distress. Love would have a more tenuous place in the overall structure of the re-formed family, though of course one would expect that it was love that brought together the newly forming couple. Another feature seems to be that at the beginning of a newly forming family the stepmother is still perceived in mythical terms, and, as in our fairy stories, more universally disliked than stepfathers. In the research of Barnes et al. (1997), they found that there was a 'general difference in attitude to stepfathers and stepmothers. Positive feelings were much more likely towards stepfathers, while strong hostility was almost entirely confined to stepmothers.'[30] So if the stepmother is to become the new norm of mother, she has to overcome the social and psychological prejudice against a 'second mother.'[31] She will need to establish herself as dependable and trustworthy and as able to create a secure attachment to her stepchildren as any biological mother. She will also need to accept that fathers or stepfathers never receive the same amount of hostility, unfair as this may seem.

At the closed doors of our psychological theories the stepmother is going to have to shout loud to be let in and challenge our attachment theories. But that is not her only task. The real life experiences of being a stepmother, from the research findings I have mentioned, all testify to the rough ride she will have from her stepchildren and from the ghost of their mother. She will never be allowed to forget that she is walking in someone else's shoes. She will also encounter conflict with the father of her stepchildren as he and his children adjust to a new life. He will be torn between loyalty to his children and a wish that his children could love his new wife as much as he does. Elizabeth Gaskell (1860) in her novel *Wives and Daughters* sagely commented, 'a stepmother to a girl is a different thing to a second wife to a man.'[32] And then there is the disillusionment all round. Many young stepmothers who are marrying for the first time a man with children have voiced the view, 'I married the man, not his children.' Finally, a stepfamily is more vulnerable to divorce than a first time marriage. Sixty per cent of second marriages end in another divorce, and so we see that whatever the advantages of 'multiple families,' they are still, at this moment, less enduring or solid.[33] One man I interviewed grew up in a family where his mother was divorced twice and his father only found happiness with his third wife.

And this brings me to perhaps the most difficult area of all, when thinking about stepparenting. I have already mentioned William Gladstone's comment that stepparenting five children was 'work far beyond human strength.'[34] And Maddox reflecting on her experience of being a stepmother in contrast to having her own children later, also corroborated Gladstone's comment, that being a stepparent '*takes more work*' (emphasis added).[35] One disconcerting fact is that for some stepparents it can be work 'beyond human strength' and I have in mind those who have been badly let down themselves when children. Their emotional development may have been disrupted by being tossed between warring parents and stepparents who themselves lacked 'human strength.' Research evidence is suggesting that 'people who were brought up in unhappy or disrupted homes are more likely . . . to make an unhappy marriage and to divorce.'[36] In the same vein, Barnes et al. (1998) wrote,

> Children whose parents had divorced were twice as likely to separate themselves as those who had lost a parent through death. And interestingly, the pattern of marital break-ups could be traced back to the grandparents' generation.[37]

On this account it is not surprising to discover that not only are second marriages less secure than expectation, but the stepparents themselves, because of their own emotional disruptions, may be ill equipped with the superhuman strength that is required to bring up someone else's child. It may be for this very reason that stepparents continue to be vilified. They have often not been up to the task.

It seems clear that the therapeutic world needs to be more willing to acknowledge that there are many stepparents and stepchildren in our society. We need to be aware of some of the emotional strains that they all undergo and offer some understanding. Stepparents need to know that the hate that they will receive from their stepchildren, such as, 'I'm not going to do what you say as you are not my mother!' will evoke deep visceral feelings within. They may well feel a mounting sense of outrage and as one stepmother said, 'My fourteen year old stepdaughter makes me angrier than I can ever remember feeling in my life except with my sister.'[38] Stepparents need help to understand that the feelings that they may have towards their stepchildren may evoke passionate feelings about other significant figures in their past, as the quotation above suggests. And in turn a stepchild's feelings towards a stepparent may be far more complicated than the rejecting tone of 'you are not my real mother!' There is research evidence suggesting that the identity of the child receives a severe blow at divorce, and the child may have years of hard work to recover its equilibrium and sense of self.[39] 'You are not my real mother' may be a first attempt of the child to sort out who they are and where they are in relationship to this second mother. And equally the stepparent needs to remember that they also are trying to work out a satisfactory relationship with their stepchild. Another seldom discussed fact that creates enormous tension in a newly formed second marriage is that stepchildren, if they are in their early adolescence when the new family is formed, may well try their best to break up the new family. All children of divorce harbour a fantasy that one day their parents will get back together again. If they are old enough their hostility to their stepparent may well be part of a conscious intention to achieve just that.[40]

As I come to the end of this chapter it seems to be clear that 'step-parenting has long been neglected in modern psychoanalytic thinking'[41] yet we are witnessing a new form of parenting that is emerging from the nuclear family matrix. Couples are re-forming themselves in new ways and some are choosing to have several partners, so we need to think about this new form of multiple childcare. Stepfamilies are not going to be helped if we continue to adhere to the model of the nuclear family as the only one that can ensure mental health. I do not think it would be an exaggeration to say that most therapists believe that it is the flowing milk from the benign mother's breast that is the essential condition for mental well-being. Having said that, I do not want to imply that we should ignore the research that is being done today upon the mental well-being of both mother and infant and how it is strengthened if breast-feeding can be managed.[42] But I do think we need to realize that this is an ideal that is beyond the experience of many. Added to which we need to begin to grasp the fact that many of the people who need help are struggling with the internal images of two fathers and two mothers, often in conflict with each other. We need to loosen the tight imaginative hold we have about the essential necessity of the mother and child at the breast and realize that multiple mothering has been much nearer the fact of the matter in child-rearing practices throughout the world over the last two centuries.[43]

We need to let into the narrow and exclusive picture we have of the internal world a much richer universe of wet nurses and nannies, grandparents and siblings, stepparents and stepsiblings, who all have played and still play a significant part in child rearing. Fonagy and Allison (2016) put it well: 'Throughout the history of psychoanalysis there has been concern that paying too much attention to consciousness and mechanisms of mind will result in an impoverished picture of the individual's psychic reality.'[44] Do we really impoverish our psychoanalytic thinking if we recognize that psychic reality and social reality combine to create the fabric of our internal world? Surely the fantasies about our parents or siblings cannot be divorced from the reality of their presence. As I have argued already, one of the difficulties that psychoanalytic theory gets into if it ignores the impact of social reality is that it becomes curiously untethered. The phrase 'it is all in the mind' has often been used to ignore the truth of what is really going on. Bettelheim's wish to show us how fairy stories were depicting the development of the infant mind necessarily had to ignore the possibility that fairy stories were a way of confronting the reality of human behaviour. Stepmothers are different from mothers both in reality and in fantasy. We make a profound category mistake if we say the feelings and fantasies we have about the stepmother are no more than the more difficult feelings we have about the mother. Apart from anything else to be a stepparent may be the most difficult role that anyone may be called upon to play, and we do them a profound disservice if we reduce the powerful feelings that they arouse to fantasies about the original parents.

Notes

1 Euripides (1963) *Medea*. Trans. P. Vellacott. London: Penguin Books.
2 Maddox (1975) p. 15. I want to thank Blue Hodgson for suggesting I read this autobiography.
3 Maddox (1975) p. 1.
4 Quoted in Maddox (1975) p. 58.
5 Maddox (1975) p. 25.
6 Wallerstein and Lewis (2007) p. 457.
7 The concept of the 'blended family' was first coined in 1972 (Merriam-Webster).
8 Popinoe (1994).
9 Barnes, Thompson, Daniel and Burchardt (1997) p. v.
10 Mead (1971) quoted in Maddox (1975) p. 31.
11 Bray and Kelly (1999) p. 12.
12 Bray and Kelly (1999) p. 263.
13 Wallerstein and Lewis (2007) p. 446.
14 Wallerstein and Lewis (2007) pp. 446–448.
15 I am grateful to Anna Hopewell who pointed out that scapegoating of a child was not a prerogative of divorcing couples.

16 Wallerstein and Lewis (2007) p. 446.
17 Wallerstein and Resnikoff (1997); see also Johnston and Roseby (1997).
18 Wallerstein, Lewis and Blakeslee (2002) p. 27.
19 Quoted in Wallerstein Lewis and Rosenthal (2013) pp. 169–170.
20 Eliot (1992 [1860]) p. 597.
21 Robinson (1991) pp. 300–301.
22 Wallerstein and Lewis (2007); see also Leach (2014) and Rutter (1991).
23 Barnes et al. (1997) pp. 14–15.
24 Wallerstein et al. (2002) p. 248.
25 Wallerstein et al. (2013). One quarter of the mothers in their twenty-five year longitudinal study were 'fragile in their psychological adjustment' and one consequence was that 'the personal lives of the children were dogged with serious problems' (pp. 178–179).
26 Wallerstein et al. (2002) p. xiii.
27 Robinson (1991) p. 147.
28 Maddox (1975) p. 181.
29 Mill (1869) p. 157.
30 Barnes et al. (1998) p. 278.
31 Coles (2015).
32 Gaskell (1996 [1860]) p. 74.
33 See Wallerstein et al. (2002) and Robinson (1991) on the vulnerability of second marriages.
34 Asquith (1936) p. 238.
35 Maddox (1975) p. 181.
36 Rutter (1991) p. 198.
37 Barnes et al. (1997) p. 285.
38 Quoted in Maddox (1975) p. 81.
39 Wallerstein and Lewis (2007).
40 Martin (2009).
41 Boston (2003) pp. 177–179.
42 Gerhardt (2004).
43 Coles (2015), Fildes (1988).
44 Fonagy and Allison (2016) p. 6.

References

Asquith, M. (1936) *The Autobiography of Margot Asquith. Vol. 1.* London: Penguin Books.
Coles, P. (2015) *The Shadow of the Second Mother: Nurses and Nannies in Theories of Development.* London/New York: Routledge.
Barnes, G., Thompson, P., Daniel, G. and Burchardt, N. (1997) *Growing Up in Stepfamilies.* Oxford: Oxford University Press.
Boston, L. (2003) Doing to being: psychological factors influencing women's experience of stepmothering. *Psychoanalytic Psychotherapy.* 20: 177–179.
Boswell, J. (1988) *The Kindness of Strangers: The Abandonment of Children in Western Europe from Later Antiquity to the Renaissance.* London: Penguin.
Bray, J.H. and Kelly, J. (1999) *Step families: Love, Marriage, and Parenting in the First Decade.* New York: Broadway Books.
Eliot, G. (1992 [1860]) *The Mill on the Floss.* London: Random House Ltd.
Fonagy, P. and Allison, E. (2016) Psychic reality and the nature of consciousness. *International Journal of Psychoanalysis.* 97. 1: 5–24.

Fildes, V. (1988) *Wet Nursing: A History from Antiquity to the Present.* Oxford: Basil Blackwell.

Gaskell, E. (1966 [1860]) *Wives and Daughters.* London: Penguin Books.

Gerhardt, S. (2004) *Why Love Matters: How Affection Shapes a Baby's Brain.* Abingdon: Routledge.

Johnston, J.R. and Roseby, V. (1997) *In the Name of the Child: A Developmental Approach to Understanding and Helping Children of Conflicted and Violent Divorce.* New York: The Free Press.

Leach, P. (2014) *Family Breakdown: Helping Children Hang On to Both Parents.* London: Unbound.

Maddox, B. (1975) *The Half-Parent: Living with Other People's Children.* London: Andre Deutsch Ltd.

Martin, W. (2009) *Stepmonster: A New Look at Why Stepmothers Think, Feel and Act the Way We Do.* Houghton, Mifflin Harcourt.

Mill, J.S. (2006 [1869]) *The Subjection of Women.* London: Penguin Books.

Popinoe P. (1994) The Evolution of Marriage and the Problem of Stepfamilies: A Biosocial Perspective. In *Stepfamilies. Who Benefits? Who Does Not?* Ed A. Booth and J. Dunn. New Jersey/Hove: Lawrence Erlbaum Assoc. Publishers.

Robinson, M. (1991) *Family Transformation through Divorce and Remarriage: A Systemic Approach.* London: Routledge.

Rutter, M. (1991) *Maternal Deprivation Reassessed.* 2nd edition. London: Penguin Books.

Wallerstein, J. and Resnikoff, D. (1997) Parental divorce and developmental progression: an inquiry into their relationship. *International Journal of Psycho-Analysis.* 78. 1: 135–155.

Wallerstein, J., Lewis, J. and Blakeslee, S. (2002) *The Unexpected Legacy of Divorce: A 25 Year Landmark Study.* London: Fusion Press.

Wallerstein, J. and Lewis, J. (2007) Sibling Outcomes and Disparate Parenting and Stepparenting after Divorce: Report from a 10-Year Longitudinal Study. *Psychoanalytical Psychology.* 24: 445–458.

Wallerstein, J., Lewis, J. and Rosenthal, S.P. (2013) Mothers and Their Children after Divorce. *Psychoanalytical Psychology.* 30. 2: 167–187.

Chapter 8

The new reality?

A constant complaint has been that psychotherapists have not kept up with the problems that confront stepfamilies and not least that they have failed to imagine what a stepparent might be going through. One stepmother wrote,

> We are likely, when faced with the difficulties of stepfamily life – rejecting stepchildren, unsupportive husbands, friends and too frequently even therapists who don't get what we are going through – to feel like failures and to internalize notions about stepmothers being cruel, uncaring, insensitive, and ignorant about children.[1]

It is a puzzling question as to why we continue to ignore stepparents.

I have been left, from all I have read about stepparents and stepchildren, with an overwhelming sense of the difficulties that families face when a marriage breaks up. Everyone is left with their confidence bruised and their hopes and ideals under scrutiny. When, out of this melting pot, new couples form bringing with them children from their previous marriages, then all hell may be let loose, as the re-constituted family settles down. Research evidence is optimistic that the majority of children do eventually get over the trauma of divorce, and while that may be the case, I want to suggest that relationships with stepparents may create conflict and dissonance in future relationships and we need to be mindful of the possibility of a stepparent transference in therapy.

In my book, *The Shadow of the Second Mother* (2015), I suggested that over the last 3,000 years it was common to find that children, whether rich or poor, were not brought up by their mother in their early years. It was only in the late eighteenth and nineteenth century that the focus on the nuclear family gripped the Western cultural imagination, and it is from this template that our psychological theories have been derived. The question I was asking then was what was the emotional effect of being fed by someone other than one's mother, and what was the nature of the attachment that was formed by these children whose earliest and most intimate experience had been at the breast or on the knee of someone who was not their mother. I found evidence from biography and autobiography that some children who had been wet nursed or had had nannies were deeply divided between the scarcely remembered attachment to their wet nurse/nanny and the mother to whom they were supposed to be devoted. One result was that many felt they could never trust a close relationship again.[2]

I do not think that children who have stepparents suffer the same type of bereavement as those who have lost their primary attachment figure such as a wet nurse or nanny. Stepparents usually enter a child's life later and are seldom a child's primary caretaker in the earliest days. However in the research I have read it seems that all members of a family that breaks up have a painful journey, though it is undoubtedly the child or children who suffer the most. The ACE study that was set up in the US in 1985 to study the health of children suggested in a recent finding that the second highest trauma a young child could suffer was from the divorce of its parents and this trauma could continue to affect its health in later life.[3] One adult reflecting on her parents' divorce said 'Was I angry with them? No. I was too sad, too bewildered to be angry.'[4] The feeling of being 'too sad' to be angry when her parents divorced was corroborated by one woman I interviewed and now describe.

Miss C. was seven when her parents divorced. She remembered crying every day for a year and to this day she cannot put into words what exactly was making her so sad, but what seems clear is that she has suffered from a lifelong depression ever since. She stayed with her mother and her siblings and her father moved away and soon married again. Her parents did not fight or argue about custody of the children, indeed Miss C. said she has continued to be puzzled about what had gone wrong in the marriage, as her parents seemed to remain on friendly terms. Her inconsolable sadness found an expression in her hatred of the countryside where her father now lived. It was flat and seemed never to come to an end and this landscape has reflected her lifelong mood. Her misery was compounded by her physical revulsion of her stepmother who was kind and did her best to be friendly to Miss C. But Miss C. felt an inward nausea, above all, at her stepmother's smell; she dreaded the goodnight kiss or her stepmother sitting on her bed reading her a bedtime story. All these feelings, like her earlier unspeakable sadness, were without a language that could be articulated, let alone shared with her parents. She just knew something was wrong, or one might say, smelt wrong, about this relationship she was being asked to manage. When Miss C. grew up she did have a few affairs with men but her sadness remained uncomforted, and she preferred to live alone. In this solitary place, she believed, there was no fear of being reminded of her sadness, or more psychologically, we might say, she feels safer against the fear of being intruded upon by someone who smells wrong.

It is interesting that Miss C. experienced her stepmother as smelling wrong, and this would seem to link to quite profound feelings of the biological strangeness of her stepmother. The idea of divorce creating new kinship structures, as mentioned in the previous chapter, raises the question about whether children can flourish in a divorced family as well as in a family where the attachment to a mother and father has not been broken. Researchers, such as Daly and Wilson (1998) who wrote a book called *The Truth About Cinderella*, suggested that from an evolutionary point of view parents are more likely to treat their natural children better than a child who does not have a genetic connection. In other words,

Miss C.'s physical revulsion when in the presence of her stepmother may have roots in a deeper fear about her safety, or in the words of Daly and Wilson, 'Having a stepparent has turned out to be the most powerful epidemiological risk factor for severe child maltreatment yet discovered.'[5] So one might say that the psychological truth about the Cinderella fairy story is that a child with a stepparent is more likely to be mistreated than the child who lives with its natural parents.

Now it is clear that Miss C. was never maltreated by her stepmother, but Daly and Wilson's work does help us to understand that the negative images we have of the stepmother and to a lesser extent the stepfather lie deeper than a cultural prejudice. They smell wrong because stepparents are not 'natural' parents in a biological sense and for this reason they will always be on a collision course with their stepchildren. Their stepchildren will seldom feel as viscerally attached to them as to their own parents. And in turn stepparents will never feel that their stepchildren are equal to their own children. In other words, the stepfamily is a fragile form of family life. This is supported by research on the much weaker affiliations between stepparents and their children. Not only do stepparents rate their role as stepparent as 'about as important as belonging to a voluntary association or having a hobby,'[6] but stepchildren will in turn feel less obligation to look after their stepparents in old age.

The fact that a stepparent can never be a 'natural' parent unleashes other psychological conflicts. Perhaps one of the most destructive factors in divorce can become centred around issues of money and inheritance, an all too familiar theme in Cinderella. One example I was given raised an interesting legal issue. Should a stepchild inherit his stepfather's favourite painting or was it rightfully the father's son who should have been left it? As the legal situation stands at the moment, both in the US and the UK, stepparents do not have legal rights or obligations over their stepchildren. At the moment a stepmother does not have any rights when a much loved stepchild is taken away because of the break-up of the marriage or partnership.[7] Similarly if a stepparent was to die intestate, their stepchildren would not be considered as part of their estate.[8] It will be interesting to see whether in time, and as stepfamilies become as familiar as monogamous marriages, the stepfamily will become a recognized legal institution, with certain well formulated rights and obligations towards stepchildren.

There is another psychological difficulty which stepfamilies encounter that centres around rivalry for attention and the uneasy rivalry for affection. Of course rivalry exists between parents and children and between parents and siblings, and problems of money and inheritance can become a major issue in any family. But following divorce and when stepparents are faced with their partner's children, a more open and extensive expression of rivalry seems to occur. A typical example will be a child who has lived alone with a parent for some years and who will naturally resent the arrival of a stepparent who demands attention. Stepparent and child will both be fighting for the exclusive love from this parent. Interestingly all the research evidence suggests that stepmothers have a worse time than stepfathers, as they are kicked in the shins by their stepchildren and exasperate their husbands with their demands that he should control his unruly child. 'Stepmother and their stepchildren are probably the most serious losers in stepfamily relationships.'[9] As in the fairy stories, again stepfathers will have an easier time.

Rivalry can also have its flames fanned by a deserted husband or wife who can encourage dissension in the newly formed family. There are some horrifying accounts of the lengths deserted partners, usually wives, will go to as they seek revenge. The favoured method is to poison the children's affection towards the partner who has left and remarried.[10] But equally the fire can be stoked by the stepchildren themselves, especially if they are adolescent. They may, unconsciously, do their best to break up this new marriage in innumerable and subtle ways. They may insist that they always choose which TV programme to watch, or which restaurant to go to, and a helpless stepparent may find she or he is silenced in the face of a partner who is facing a conflict of loyalty between a new partner and a natural child.[11] In the many self-help books that have been written, there are painful examples of how to manage the rivalry that will be occasioned when a stepparent steps into the hallowed ground of a parent/child relationship, and stepparents will be counselled not to demand too much attention from their new spouse as the fight for who is loved best finds a resolution.[12]

There are other interesting parallels with Miss C. and the view that Daly and Wilson bring to the stepparenting conflict. In Chapter 6, I briefly looked at an account I had been given by a colleague of the breakdown of a therapy. I am now wondering whether the texture of this therapy may have revoked something like Miss C's sense that her stepmother smelt wrong. Could this metaphor of smell be another way of describing why the therapy with the businessman ended when he began to express discomfort over the session times and the physical layout of the room. In Daly and Wilson's work they suggest an inevitable genetic dissonance between parenting and stepparenting, and so we could imagine this businessman might have been getting in touch with a memory of the feelings he had when he encountered his stepmother. His stepmother looked wrong, and he was beginning to have the same feelings about his therapist's room. This is a conflict that naturally occurs between a stepmother and her stepchild because she can never, biologically or psychologically, take the place of the mother. There is always something that smells wrong or looks wrong or feels wrong; in the words of Gerhardt (2010), '[s]mells provide basic information about what is safe and familiar, and what is not. The sense of smell is thought to be the foundation of our mammalian emotional systems in the brain.'[13]

In the second case that I cite in Chapter 7, of the woman who described the breakdown of a second therapy that she had sought after the death of her lover, she had wondered why she felt so angry with her therapist and came to realize that both the therapist and the stepmother spoke a 'foreign' language. That is to say neither of them spoke English as their first language. The foreign mother tongue linked the therapist to the stepmother and reminded this woman of her unhappiness and anger when her mother died and was replaced by a stepmother. What may have augmented the tension was that this second therapist was also a step-therapist in comparison to the first therapist. Here again, I want to suggest, there was a breakdown in the therapy because of a complicated transference that linked the therapist to the stepmother and possibly the previous therapist. This transference had the feeling that the language was wrong. In these three cases, Miss C. expressed her anger and dismay with her stepmother through the metaphor of smell, the businessman through the metaphor of his therapist's room looking wrong, and the woman I interviewed expressed her distress through the metaphor of her therapist speaking a foreign language. All these metaphors suggest that an undiagnosed stepparent transference can evoke visceral feelings that something is wrong. There is almost universal agreement between researchers that children are traumatized by divorce, so it would be unsurprising if this trauma and the arrival of stepparents was not a major feature of therapy from time to time.

Most research suggests that the majority of children do recover from their bewildered sadness following a divorce, and that they do catch up emotionally with more securely attached children a bit later in life.[14] It is only the bottom twenty-five per cent of children who are left struggling with self-defeating strategies in later life and what is significant about this group is that they are the ones who came from a dysfunctional family in the first place and before the divorce took place. Yet as in all attempts to make a definitive statement about the effect of divorce on children, even those who are confident in the long-term resilience of most children do acknowledge that children of divorce do less well at school, may have health issues throughout their life and tend to leave home early.[15] And a Finnish research found that depression and violent death in men was associated with divorce and separation.[16] It was small comfort to a woman, whose parents had divorced when she was twelve, to be told she was lucky because now she would have two mothers.

> I was twelve and at boarding school, desperately miserable about what was going on at home, especially the brand new stepmother who'd arrived in dad's house. The school matron caught me crying and I confided this to her. Do you know what she said? She said 'you are really lucky to have two mothers.'[17]

I met one person, Mr A., who thought he was lucky to have two mothers, which is interesting in itself, especially in light of the research that suggests that boys may be more permanently damaged by divorce than girls, such as in the Finnish study quoted above. Mr A.'s parents divorced when he was seven and his stepparents had been 'brilliant.' His parents he described as 'introverted intellectuals' who seemed to argue the whole time. When they separated there was an equitable agreement that Mr A. should be shared between them. He was an only child. He stayed four nights with his mother and three with his father. In the beginning it was a difficult and lonely time for Mr A. He missed his friends at the weekend and was concerned about his sad mother. Things changed for him when both his parents found new partners and he suddenly found himself with a 'brilliant stepfather' who loved playing football and doing other sporting activities with Mr A. unlike his father. They became 'best friends.' Equally his stepmother was much less anxious than his own mother. She had time to cook delicious meals and read him stories and was altogether a much more lively and engaging person. In conclusion Mr A. was thankful that his parents had separated and that he had had an experience of being alongside life enhancing stepparents.

Mr A. thought that his parents' divorce had liberated his parents, but by the end of our interview I was less sure whether the good relationships he had had with his stepparents had helped him to manage close relationships in his adult life. The belief that divorce can liberate men and women was certainly well argued in J.S. Mill's (1866) persuasive essay on *The Subjection of Women*. In this essay he set out his beliefs that once women were liberated from the shackles of a marriage in which they had no legal or civil rights, men and women would find themselves at last on a more equal footing and as a consequence marriages might become happier.[18] Mr A. seemed to agree with Mill and he felt that divorce had liberated his entire family. Both his parents were happier in their second marriages and he had gained two helpful surrogate parents to whom he was devoted.

Mr A.'s experience of his parents' liberation is by no means unique even though he was the only stepchild I interviewed who felt this way. Margaret Robinson (1991), quoted in the previous chapter, was writing from the position of being a stepmother, and she believed that shared parenting not only can give some respite but also can 'bring greater objectivity.'[19] A more recent and thoughtful book on the difficulties of being a stepparent, *Stepmonster*, was written by Wednesday Martin (2015), who was quite openly addressing the problems she had faced in the early years of being a stepmother. At the same time she interviewed many other stepmothers in her pursuit of the wish to help them through the early years of a remarriage. By the end of the book she confidently wrote, 'after about five years, remarriages with children are actually stronger, happier, and more likely to last than first marriages.'[20] One important characteristic of such a strong second marriage was emphasized in Church's (2004) research in which she found that the successful stepmother does not see herself in maternal competition with the mother of her stepchildren but as an aunt. She quoted from one woman who said she saw herself as 'a close aunt, a close relative . . . The love and the relationship is there . . . I feel that keeps it clean and clear. So nobody gets confused and nobody has to get jealous.'[21] This idea of the stepmother seeing herself as an aunt was corroborated by one man I interviewed who had had in fact two stepmothers. What distinguished his second stepmother was that she did not try to be the perfect mother to her stepchildren. They came and went as they pleased and he felt that she always had an open door. What needs to be noted here however is that this man and his siblings were grown up and not dependent upon a stepmother for their care. Nevertheless he spoke warmly about his second stepmother and he felt she was open-hearted and accepting and they continue to this day to have a good relationship.

It seems clear that most stepmothers do find happiness in their stepfamilies, and most stepchildren find a way of accommodation to the new circumstances, yet I found that the stepchildren I talked to found it difficult to be totally accepting of their stepparents. Stepparents seemed to remain a thorn in their side, though some were more painful thorns than others. In contrast most stepmothers I interviewed were more positive about their experience and most felt that they had strong and enduring relationships with their stepchildren. These two points of view may be confounded at first if we go back to Mr A. I did not doubt his belief that he felt he had benefited from his parents' second marriages. It was only later and on reflection that I privately questioned Mr A.'s optimism. I had not asked him about his present life and he only mentioned in passing that he had had three failed marriages. He seemed unwilling to talk about these relationships and this left me with the impression that there was a subterranean pain that was only partially glimpsed when he told me that he had had six children with whom he had minimum contact. I was left with the sense that in his heart he was still the sad and lonely child of seven who had felt cast adrift when his parents parted. It had been good that in his childhood he no longer had to hear his parents arguing and this was followed by kind stepparents, but in spite of all this his three marriages and his attenuated relationship with his six children spoke of an extensive hurt following his parents' divorce. He was, I think, communicating that his own confidence had foundered and that he did not know how best to manage difficulties. This must be one of the most painful things to acknowledge as a stepparent; you can be as good a stepparent as any parent, but too often it is still not enough to heal the previous wounds.

Psychologically one might say that Mr A.'s three marriages seemed to reflect an internalized model of parents who were ill equipped to sort out their differences. Or put another way he had repeated a model of how to sort out conflict. You walk out. This early impression was not effaced by the remarriage of his parents and his good relationship with his stepparents. I found myself wondering, if Mr A. was to come into therapy today, how I might imagine that his stepparents would feature? In the first place I would be much more alert to the probability that feelings about both sets of parents and stepparents were intertwined and split. I could, for instance, imagine that the early days of therapy might be characterized as 'brilliant,' as though I was a stepparent, livening up his life. In this honeymoon period I might be imagined as helping him to leave behind forever his distressed feelings about his sad mother and angry feelings about his disappointing father. As the therapy deepened in significance, however, we might get to the lonely little boy who felt neglected by his arguing parents. His disappointment and rage and distress may then come to the fore. At this moment he might begin to question the foundations of therapy, he might begin to feel angry and that I was not to be trusted, that I 'smelt' wrong and that I was just out to upset him. What might come crashing down was our 'brilliant' beginning as it began to show cracks. At that moment he might walk out, unless of course I could find a way of helping him to see that his 'brilliant' stepparents had helped him and were extremely important but had not been able to reach the sad and lonely little boy whom now we were facing.

I hope in this imagined example I have made clear that the fragility of the 'brilliant' stepparent transference needs to be acknowledged as life enhancing; but if and when other emotions began to surface, Mr A. would have needed help to face a deeper wound. He needed to find a way of accepting that his parents' love for each other had failed and this had left him feeling wounded and ignored. What I hope to have illustrated is that in the case of Mr A. his stepparents were an important presence in his life and furthermore I would have expected that they would have been there in the therapy. It would only have been when the therapy deepened and other emotions began to surface that the stepparent transference would have needed to be peeled back to allow the more painful feelings about his parents to reach the light of day. It needs to be noted that in my speculation I am imagining that in the first instance I would be confronted with a stepparent transference and only later would our relationship reveal the more heartbroken little boy. This is in contrast to the two cases I have already mentioned, where the stepparent transference only appears later in the therapy.

I was left quite disquieted when I thought about Mr A.'s six children with whom he had lost contact, and this then led me to wonder whether divorce has liberated men and women as J.S. Mill so passionately believed would be the case. Our divorce laws have relieved men and women from enduring a living hell together when the relationship breaks down, but has it liberated our children? If, as I believe, an indelible footprint is left in the psyche of children whose families have broken up, have we been too sanguine that children will get over their family break-up? It seems to me that we may have not taken sufficient account of the circular effect of divorce upon children. Or put another way, the imprint of divorce can leave children with a model that relational difficulties are best dealt with by divorce and so the divorce solution augments and re-enforces itself.

The repeating pattern of divorce finds a good explanation in the idea that patterns of malfunctioning can be repeated in the next generation if they remain unrecognized: 'In every nursery there are ghosts. They are visitors from the unremembered past of the parents; the uninvited guests at the christening.'[22] Fraiberg's wonderful image emerged from her understanding of the way neglected or abused children could become neglecting and abusing parents, if they were not helped to recognize that they were repeating the pattern of their own suffering upon their children. If, as now seems to be the case, a new kinship system of stepfamilies is emerging, we need to consider the idea that there may be unrecognized repercussions upon the psyche of children of divorce if the unremembered past of stepparents is not taken into consideration. At the very least, divorce creates a split in the child's psyche, and the anger and disappointment with a mother or father can be projected onto an 'evil' stepmother or stepfather, or in the case of Mr A. above, onto 'brilliant' stepparents and denigrated parents.

The social reality that confronts every child of divorce is that they have to find a way of integrating two sets of families with their different stories and heritage and in turn our psychological theories have also to find a way of thinking about the new configuration of family life and its effects upon the psyche. For instance, if we go back to the Oedipus myth, when he came to the cross roads, it was not a simple cross roads; there were other metaphorical roads that led to the point where Laius pushed him out of the way and Oedipus killed him. Oedipus had already experienced the anxiety of a father who wanted him dead, a mother who colluded with her husband and abandoned him, a shepherd who had saved his life and finally a man and woman who looked after him and would have him believe that they were his real parents. These were some of the social and emotional forces in the dramatic life of Oedipus as imagined by Sophocles.[23] But if we use Sophocles' drama as a metaphoric description of the complicated threads that can make up a life where parents have parted with their child, we have a delicate task to unravel the social reality and its pressures from the way these experiences are configured in fantasy and the unconscious. Oedipus' search for the truth needs the support of a society that will tell things as they are. Mr A. in his three marriages seemed to have been searching for a vanishing dream of a constant loving presence, but he stood at a cross road, split between his loyalty to his 'brilliant' stepparents and his disappointing parents. There was no one to tell him the truth that divorce can split the psyche as one tries to master where one's true parents lie, and instead he inflicted his traumatic search upon the next generation, his six children.

So what I am suggesting is that we need to take stepparents as serious contributors to the psychological and social life of a child, but now we need to add that stepparents will be bringing their own intergenerational history to their stepfamily. This adds enormous complexity to the family situation but it might also help us to understand why children of divorce are more likely to divorce in adult life. Unfortunately it is not uncommon to find that many stepparents are not up to the job. They may have grown up in dysfunctional families that left them with a long-lasting fear of close relationships. They may have found conflict too stressful to manage and it was this that precipitated them to leave their first marriage. Their second marriage may prove to be no better if they have not had the opportunity to reflect upon their contribution to their marital difficulties. It is in this way that divorce repeats itself across the generations.[24]

I interviewed Mrs L. who had married a divorced man when she was in her early twenties. He brought to the marriage a five-year-old daughter who lived with her mother but spent weekends and some holidays with her father and Mrs L. Mrs L as a young and expectant bride was in a difficult position. She was in love with her husband and the last thing she wanted at weekends was a child of five who hated her and got in the way of the precious time she so much desired with her husband. This difficulty is familiar to many women who have been in the same position as Mrs L. when they marry a man who already has a child. Mrs L. was a naturally kind woman who loved children but this situation was beyond anything she had imagined. She had not expected to be kicked in the shins and told 'You're not my mother so I am not going to do what you want!'

Now at a distance of twenty years there were several things that Mrs L. could reflect upon. She had never asked herself why her husband's first marriage had failed and why five years later her marriage to him also failed. She realized now that his own deprived and violent upbringing had left him with little internal impression of a loving and kind relationship. The abusive behaviour he had known in childhood had left him with an unsatisfied longing for a maternal figure who would soothe his pain, and Mrs L. had imagined that she could woo him and heal his wounds. The inevitable disappointment he experienced when his needs were not perfectly met left him angry with Mrs L. and she discovered too late, and after she had had his two daughters, that she could not change him.

I think that Mrs L's experience illustrates several things about the burden that a stepmother can carry. Her stepdaughter was already a troubled child who had witnessed her father's violent behaviour towards her mother. This would have distorted the child's feelings towards her stepmother and when she kicked Mrs L. in the shins she may well have been venting some of her distressed and angry feelings towards her father that she would have been too frightened to have acknowledged. There was another difficulty Mrs L. brought to this marriage. She had come from an intact family in which conflicts had been managed and sorted out, so she was ill equipped to manage a dysfunctional man and a distressed stepdaughter. The model she had internalized was that a good enough family could sort out its problems. In her marriage she discovered she was always working against the grain, as it were. She imagined difficulties could be thought about and discussed rather than acted out with abusive behaviour, but her husband had only known the resolution of family difficulties through violence.

Here we get a glimpse of how intergenerational experiences get repeated in the next generation, unwittingly and unconsciously. I am sure Mrs L.'s husband will have started out his second marriage with hope, but the tragedy was that in spite of the healing forces of Mrs L.'s natural love for children and for her husband she was not able to contain his disrupting behaviour when he was distressed and angry. The legacy of this unhappy marriage has left marks on all who were involved. Mrs L.'s husband lives on his own, cut off from his children, and one suspects profoundly depressed. Mrs L. has had her confidence severely knocked and now she doubts her own capacity to choose a man who would be loving and kind. Her stepdaughter, with whom she now has a friendly but attenuated relationship, has never settled down and remains single. Finally we could speculate that the turmoil of Mrs L.'s failed marriage will have been carried over onto her two daughters and we might expect that they will have a hard journey to find a man whom they can trust.

Mrs L. is only one case but I think it does raise a question as to whether, if we became more active in thinking about divorce and stepparenting, we could encourage our children to think about their potential partner in a more psychologically sophisticated way. There used to be a cliché that was told to men, look at your future mother-in-law for you will see how your wife will be in years to come.

Today, in the new kinship system of remarriage we are seeing, we may need to say to our children, look at your partner's previous marriages/relationships, and ask what went wrong before you marry. We are more sure nowadays that the early relationships of childhood cloud our feelings and perceptions. Early difficulties in childhood will affect future relationships and Mrs L.'s husband was a good case in point. He had known violence in his childhood and had been put into care, so that as a young man his longing for a good and loving relationship will have been hard to achieve. It is for this reason that the greater knowledge we have about our future partner's past relationships will alert us to the conflicts we may encounter.

In spite of all the reassuring research that I have read that children recover from divorce, I am still left with the thought that children are the least considered when it comes to marriage break-up and yet they are the ones who are hurt the most by divorce. I now find myself in a quandary. I have come to the conclusion that stepparents are a much discounted and neglected group in our psychological thinking and we need to give them more of our psychological time, as they seem to be an important part of the family structures of today. It is only by turning to self-help books that one gets any idea of how painful the early days of a remarriage with children, whether your own, your partners,' or both, will be. Stepparents, in these books, are screaming out that it is a living hell in the early days and it was the realization that I had not thought about them in my therapeutic practice that prompted me to start this book and I hope that all I have written will show that I have appreciated how painful the task of stepparenting can be as new affiliations and loyalties are forged.

Notes

1 Martin (2015) p. 24.
2 Coles (2015).
3 https://acestoohigh.com.
4 Leach (2014).
5 Daly and Wilson (1998 p. 7). Dickens (1850) provides a description of the risk factor of a stepfather in his portrait of Mr Murdstone in *David Copperfield*. 'If I have an obstinate horse or dog to deal with . . . I beat him . . . I make him wince, and smart. I say to myself "I'll conquer that fellow"; and if it were to cost him all the blood he had I should do it.' And he terrifies David into submission (pp. 48–49).
6 White (1994) p. 111.
7 *Guardian Family* (16 April 2016). The article was called 'My stepson who I loved – and lost.' It concerned a young stepmother whose marriage broke up after five years, but during that time she had grown to love her stepson who was three when she first met him. As she says, 'In a split second, any rights I had to love you were taken away.'
8 White (1994) p. 111.
9 Zill (1994) p. 131.
10 LeBey (2005).
11 Martin (2015).
12 Bray and Kelly (1998).
13 Gerhardt (2010) p. 59.

14 Wallerstein, Lewis and Blakeslee (2002).
15 Bray and Kelly (1998), Gorell Barnes et al. (1998), Hetherington and Kelly (2002), Martin (2015), Wallerstein et al. (2002).
16 Quoted in Leach (2014) p. xviii.
17 Leach (2014) p. xviii.
18 Mill (1869).
19 Robinson (1991) p. 147.
20 Martin (2015) p. 249.
21 Church (2004) p. 257.
22 Fraiberg (1987) p. 100.
23 Sophocles (1962).
24 Bray and Kelly (1998).

References

ACE. (Adverse Childhood Experiences) Available at https://acestoohigh.com.
Booth, A. and Dunn, J. (1994) Eds. *Stepfamilies: Who Benefits? Who Does Not?* New Jersey: Lawrence Erlbaum Associates Inc.
Bray, J.H. and Kelly, J. (1998) *Stepfamilies: Love, Marriage, and Parenting in the First Decade.* New York: Broadway Books.
Chodorow, N. (1978) *The Reproduction of Mothering.* California/London: University of California Press.
Coles, P. (2011) *The Uninvited Guest from the Unremembered Past.* London: Karnac.
Coles, P. (2015) *The Shadow of the Second Mother.* London/New York: Routledge.
Church, E. (2004) *Understanding Stepmothers: Women Share Their Struggles, Successes, and Insights.* Toronto: HarperCollins Publishers Ltd.
Daly, M. and Wilson, M. (1998) *The Truth About Cinderella: A Darwinian View of Parental Love.* London: Weidenfeld & Nicholson.
Dickens, C. (1994 [1850]) *David Copperfield.* London: Penguin Books.
Fraiberg, S. (1987) *Selected Writings of Selma Fraiberg.* Ed. L. Fraiberg. Columbus: Ohio State University Press.
Gerhardt, S. (2010) *The Selfish Society: How We All Forgot to Love One Another and Made Money Instead.* London: Simon & Schuster UK Ltd.
Gerhardt, S. (2017) The Selfish Society: The State of Things. In *The Political Self: Understanding the Social Context for Mental Illness.* Ed. R. Tweedy. London: Karnac Books Ltd.
Gorell Barnes, G., Thompson, T., Daniel, G. and Burchardt, N. (1998) *Growing Up in Stepfamilies.* Oxford: Clarendon Press.
Hetherington, E.M. and Jodl, K.M. (1994) Stepfamilies as Settings for Child Development. In Booth, A. and Dunn, J. *Stepfamilies: Who Benefits? Who Does Not?* New Jersey: Lawrence Erlbaum Associates Inc.
Hetherington, E.M. and Kelly, J. (2002) *For Better or for Worse: Divorce Reconsidered.* New York/London: W.W. Norton & Co.
Leach, P. (2014) *Family Breakdown.* London: Unbound.
LeBey, B. (2005) *Re-Married with Children.* New York/Canada/Australia/London: Bantam Books.
Martin, W. (2015) *Stepmonster: A New Look at Why Real Stepmothers Think, Feel and Act the Way We Do.* Boston: Houghton Mifflin Harcourt.

Mill, J.S. (1869) *On Liberty and the Subjection of Women.* London: Penguin Classics.

Nielsen, L. (2014) Shared Physical Custody – Summary of 40 Studies on Outcomes for Children. Available at https://sharedparenting.wordpress.com/2014/11/04/51/.

Robinson, M. (1991) *Family Transformation through Divorce and Remarriage: A Systemic Approach.* London/New York: Routledge.

Sophocles (1962) *Oedipus the King.* Trans. H.D.F. Kitto. Oxford: Oxford University Press.

Wallerstein, J., Lewis, J. and Blakeslee, S. (2002) *The Unexpected Legacy of Divorce: A 25 Year Landmark Study.* London: Fusion Press.

White, L. (1994) Stepfamilies Over the Life Course: Social Support. In Booth, A. and Dunn, J. *Stepfamilies: Who Benefits? Who Does Not?* Boston: Lawrence Erlbaum Associates Inc.

Zill, N. (1994) Understanding Why Children in Stepfamilies Have More Learning and Behaviour Problems than Children in Nuclear Families. In Booth, A. and Dunn, J. *Stepfamilies: Who Benefits? Who Does Not?* New Jersey: Lawrence Erlbaum Associates Inc.

Chapter 9
Epilogue

I said in my Introduction that I have been left with some more general questions about the extent of stepparenting in our society. Or put another way, why have we become such a divorce-prone society? One answer might be that we are living in what Gerhardt (2017) has called 'a selfish society,' precipitated by the ideals of materialism that underpin the values of global capitalism.[1] Or, to extend Sandel's (2012) view in *What Money Can't Buy*, are we dominated by the prevailing belief that money can buy anything we desire? Perhaps our divorce rate is so high because we perceive our intimate relationships with others as commodities that we can get rid of when they have passed their 'sell by' dates?[2]

There is another question about the values that underpin our 'selfish society.' Maybe these values do not just lie in the hands of reckless bankers and greedy entrepreneurs. Maybe our psychological theories have also contributed to the 'selfish' society. This may seem far-fetched, but in our work that is focused on personal conflict, in the here and now, we may have unwittingly contributed to the belief that the pursuit of personal well-being can leave out of account the impact we have on our wider society and the demands we make upon the depleting resources of the natural world. It is certainly not the intention of therapy to support such a limited outlook, and it is certainly hoped that if we can understand better our own unconscious mind we will be less concerned with our own selfish needs. But nevertheless the practice of psychoanalysis does reflect the values of a society. When I was training to become a therapist, you could not openly state that you were a homosexual, as at that time it was popularly believed to be a pathology. Now you could not be turned away from a training on the basis of your sexual orientation. Here is an example of psychoanalytic thinking shifting under political pressure. If we return to Sandel's critique of our modern society in which we want to believe that money can buy anything we desire, our psychological practice does help to underpin this belief as it is only through a money transaction that we can today, for the most part, gain some insight into ourselves.

Another example of the way our psychological theories are underpinned by the values of our society can be found by comparing the value that is given to group therapy in contrast to individual therapy. Group therapy has never been held in the same esteem as individual therapy. One implied reason is that group therapy does not get to the heart of the individual matter. However the recent research that has developed from attachment theory suggests that we are social beings who can only flourish in relationships with other people. Group therapy might challenge the prevailing view of the importance of individual therapy and may help us to see ourselves in wider relief. It may also be offering an important insight into the way the 'selfish society' has grown out of our neglect of the human need to feel a responsible part of a group.

This example leads into another question concerning our psychological beliefs. There has been a tendency to cast such beliefs in tablets of stone, and there has been a reluctance to acknowledge that they are in a dialectical exchange with the beliefs of our culture. If we could be open to the social changes that are taking place in family life this might give us the space to consider whether, unintentionally, the pursuit of individual self-discovery may have contributed to the society we find ourselves in today. Furthermore, it might allow us to reconsider whether our divorce-prone society is bowing under the social values of our materialistic society and think again about the effect this may be having on the next generation.

I have found myself imagining that if there was more psychological interest and greater social awareness of the pain and hell that remarriage with young children can bring to all concerned, might the divorce rates shift? It seems to me that we have been unaware of the cauldron of fury that accompanies a second marriage. Might our views about divorce change if we were better informed? I am not saying that marriage is sacrosanct and there should be no divorce, but I wonder whether there has been enough social and economic support for families with young children. At such times, marriage is not easy. If there was more understanding, that was underpinned by a psychological appreciation of the needs of the child, and there was a greater appreciation of the stresses that children and work put upon a young couple's relationship, then divorce might not be such a popular solution to the inevitable tensions that spread out across the early years of child rearing. Furthermore, from the interviews that I have carried out, I have been surprised to discover the long-term loneliness that divorced parents can face, and this is seldom thought about in the heat of a divorce.

The question of long-term loneliness was raised for me when I interviewed a woman in her eighties who shared with me her melancholy regrets that she now had, following her divorce forty years before. 'I have no family life. All my children get together in their father's house with his second wife, and I have nothing!' She later said, 'If only I had known!' At the time of her divorce she had been an attractive woman. She was rich and privileged and had several children who were looked after by a nanny. Her husband was a prosperous workaholic and she felt lonely. Not surprisingly she had fallen in love with another man and decided to walk out of the family and leave her children with her husband and nanny. He married again and his new wife was a good enough stepmother. Not all the children liked her, but she proved to be an enduring presence. It has to be said that it is unusual for a woman to walk out on her marriage and leave her children behind, but this elderly woman's story raises the question as to whether we need to be more alert to the needs of couples when they are in difficulty. When she said to me, 'If only I had known!' one is tempted to feel she might have been helped by talking to someone about her difficulties.[3]

In another interview with a woman who was also well into her eighties, she told me, by contrast to the woman above, how she was 'rescued,' her words, from divorce by her father. She had shared with her parents that she was thinking about divorcing her husband. She had at that time three young children under the age of five. And her father said to her something along the lines, 'You made your nest and now you have to lie in it.' He also added, 'Remind yourself of why you married him in the first place. What was it you liked about him?' And with those words ringing in her mind she went home and decided to stay and make her 'nest' more comfortable. She said to me she was eternally thankful for her father's words, and her marriage had turned around and had been good enough.[4]

These differing accounts raise other questions. It is easy to react to the last story as though it was about another time and another place. We have moved on, many might say, and why counsel a woman who is unhappy to stay with a husband who does not seem to notice her? But though this woman was speaking about her own personal distress, there are marital difficulties that are not unique to her situation. Current statistics on marriage and divorce show that a first marriage is most vulnerable in its first ten years and following the birth of children. This is the time when most marriages break up.[5] So, even though it was fifty years ago, when this woman spoke to her parents, her father was reflecting a psychological truth that it is corroborated by recent research. The early years of marriage, with young children, are the most difficult time for young couples. We might even go so far as to say that universally there will be fantasies during the first ten years of marriage with children of getting out and getting free.

We could reflect even further about what the father, above, said; we could say that he was counselling his daughter to stay in her marriage because he knew that her difficulties would pass as her children grew up, even though he said no such thing. Was he implicitly suggesting that the breaking up of her marriage might leave her sad and lonely and regretful later? All the people I have interviewed, who have divorced, have expressed sadness and regret and guilt, that never leaves the newfound happiness of a second marriage.

One of the most heart-rending accounts I have read was expressed by Rachel Cusk (2012) in her book *Aftermath*. She explored the spiralling repercussions that followed her decision to ask her husband for a divorce after ten years of marriage and with two young daughters. She came to realize that her post-divorced state was a 'new reality' that was 'broken.'[6] She not only sank into anorexic depression but she looked at her two daughters and 'when my children cry a sword is run through my heart. Yet it is I who am also the cause of their crying. And for a while I am undone by this contradiction, by the difficulty of connecting the person who acted out of self-interest with the heart-broken mother who has succeeded her.'[7]

Cusk's conflict seemed to conjure up the dilemma that many young men and women are facing today. Should they pursue their self-interest and get out of their marriage? If they do, as Cusk describes, then a broken heart may follow when they see their children's distress. Gerhardt (2017) expresses that dilemma slightly differently by posing the idea that our personal self-interest intersects with the values of our 'selfish society.' Self-interest and our 'selfish society' go hand in hand in supporting material growth and the exploitation of natural resources.[8] We need to turn to the 'heartbroken mother' who is the one who needs our empathy and care. We must find a way of re-valuing our natural resources, whether mother-care or the external environment, so that we have a greater possibility of survival in a world that at times seems intent on destruction of all that matters most for human well-being.[9]

Another way of addressing this heartbreak was Leach's (2014) book, *Family Breakdown*. She makes clear that she is not advocating that couples should stay together for the sake of the children, but on the other hand she seems to be suggesting that our present divorce culture does not further the well-being of our children. One of the ills that besets families today is that they are floundering in the face of the belief that their own personal happiness should come first. We are living in a 'me culture,' she suggests.[10]

A further question led me to wonder whether our present 'me culture' is a direct result of all the legislation that has in theory been in the interests of bringing about more equal rights between men and women? Has this legislation obscured the fact that men and women are profoundly different, both psychologically and biologically, and have we failed to recognize that in this sense men and women are unequal? This is an enormously complicated area that lies at the heart of much feminist debate today, and to follow some of the fascinating arguments from Mary Wollstonecraft to Anne Brontë to Elizabeth Gaskell to Marina Warner to Nancy Chodorow to Estella Welldon, authors who have deeply affected my thinking, would involve another book. Instead I shall do no more than reiterate some of the points that I made in Chapter 3, that I called 'The strangely shaped footprint of women.' There I briefly sketched out my sense that women have found some way of freeing themselves from the legacy of patriarchal authority through cunning, or story-telling, but paradoxically has that merely increased men's fear of women?

One way of thinking further about that question is to turn to the challenging thesis in Amber Jacob's (2017) *Rethinking Matricide*.[11] What she helps us to see is that psychoanalytic theory needs to think back into the maternal, with the mother no longer an idealized or denigrated figure, or 'an object' in the unconscious, but as a figure who counteracts the male desire to be the one who is the most creative. She illustrates her thesis by taking the myth of the birth of Athena whose mother Metis was swallowed by Zeus, and then disappears from the tale while Zeus triumphantly gives birth to Athena out of his head. Jacob wishes to find a way in which Metis is brought back into our psychological understanding and our unconscious mind, bringing with her the interdiction that men must allow women to have a place in the world, alongside them but with their different way of thinking and seeing the world. Then perhaps men need not swallow women up in their anxiety to rule the universe. It is not appropriate here to go further into the subtle way Jacob embraces the Freudian concept of the unconscious mind and argues for the need to bring the mother/Metis from out of Zeus' stomach, but her ideas have helped me to think about what continues to make our present 'new reality' so difficult for the relationship between men and women.

So to return to the question of divorce, one of the tragic facts that follows on from divorce is that fathers often give up and disappear; they are described by LeBey (2005) as 'fade out fathers' because they often find the guilt at leaving their children too hard to bear.[12] If they marry again, they may find themselves unable to straddle the two worlds of their ex-marriage and their new marriage and the conflicted loyalties to their own children and their stepchildren. So if we were to imagine the case of the elderly woman interviewed above, whose father told her to go home and lie in the nest she had made, today she would be more likely to go home to a mother and stepfather, or father and stepmother. And that raises the question, have these 'fade out fathers' allowed stepfathers to take their place? And do stepfathers have the same emotional authority as the father? We know, all too painfully, that children confronted with either a stepmother or stepfather will angrily say 'I am not going to do what you say, as you are not my real father/mother!' So it is not hard to imagine that if the elderly woman, interviewed above, had been told by her stepfather to go back to the nest she had already made, she might well feel, what right has he to say that to me, when he so clearly had left his nest.

All the research evidence suggests that children need fathers or good stepfathers. Indeed fathers are probably more important for adolescent sons than mothers. But girls can feel equally devastated when fathers seem to give up on them. One case I read was of a young woman whose parents divorced when she was twenty. Her father simply disappeared out of her life. He reappeared for her graduation and her wedding, but it was 'very awkward and unpleasant for everyone.' Five years into her marriage she was now considering divorce. She was angry with her father for walking out on her life, but she also said 'I'm angry with my mother for cheating me out of a father.' This is an interesting comment by the child of a divorce, that she feels both her parents have betrayed her. Most often one parent is blamed and the other is exonerated. However in her last words it is the father's desertion that is most to blame. 'I keep thinking the scars of losing my father for so long have probably led to my own inability to make my marriage work.'[13]

But not all fathers are 'fade out fathers.' One father whose marriage had broken down and had custody of his daughter is reported to have said 'Fatherhood is evolving' and by that he seemed to mean that fathers were taking on more responsibility for caring for their children and were not just relying on 'women for the nuts and bolts of childcare.'[14] However this wish for fatherhood to evolve into greater participation in the care of their children has at times led to extremes.

When Penelope Leach (2014) wrote her book, *Family Breakdown*, she received quite vociferous criticism from the organization *New Fathers 4 Justice*. Her sensible and helpful book addressed primarily the psychological needs of a young child when a family breaks up. This led her to say that in the first three years of a child's life the child needed one home and one bed, and therefore spending three nights with one parent and four with the other was not in the best interest of the small child. This was based upon sound psychological and neurological research evidence that a child needs a secure base in these formative years if it is to form lasting attachments. However she was accused of threatening fathers from their right to share in the upbringing of their child and what was forgotten was that she was thinking first about the needs of the child.

Ian Maxwell, who founded *New Fathers 4 Justice*, was angry that fathers were being treated as less important to their children than mothers and one of the difficulties of this dispute is that of course he is right; all the evidence is that fathers are just as important as mothers and without the role model of a father many children collapse into delinquent behaviour.[15] But the argument about whether a small child, under three years of age, is best cared for by one parent when there is a divorce, can all too easily lead back into a dispute that is more concerned with what is best for the parent than what is best for the child. Of course the devoted father is heartbroken if he does not see as much of his child as the mother. What happens to the bedtime story that he has been used to reading to his child? And who will get up in the night if the child cries? How can a father ignore the echoing cries of 'I want my Daddy!'? Only with extreme anguish if he is an ordinary loving father. But against that, if the psychological evidence of attachment theory and the understanding of the neurological development of the infant brain are to be believed, the best interests of the child are served by the security of one home, one bed and one familiar caretaker being constantly around, during the first three years of life. It is an impossible dilemma for a father if he feels that at this vulnerable moment in his child's life he must leave his wife and child or his wife has asked him to go.

Fathers 4 Justice, who have criticized Leach, have received support from the detailed and lengthy research by Nielsen (2011) on the question as to whether very young children, under the age of three or four, thrive better with shared parenting after a divorce, rather than those who live with one parent and visit the other.[16] They would dispute Leach's findings and suggest that shared parenting leads to less conflict for the child, except in the cases where there is high conflict, violence, or the father is in other ways not to be trusted.

A further question that arises from this dispute is about early shared parenting, following divorce. This idea finds interesting support in Nancy Chodorow's groundbreaking book *The Reproduction of Mothering* (1978). In her 'Afterword' she looks forward to a time when equal parenting will begin to shift a social system in which the burden of childcare has rested upon the mother. Her view is illuminated by considerations of the pre-industrial family in which '[h]usband and wife, with their own and/or other children, were a cooperative producing unit' in contrast to the present day capitalist society that has 'removed grown children, grandparents, and nonfamily members from the household and sharply curtailed men's participation in family life.'[17] It is hard not to be seduced into a nostalgic dream of an extended family, with parenting shared across the generations and the sexes. I know I imagined living in a community when my children were young, and I longed to gain help and support from those who knew more and would be there to share the exhausting demands of small children. But these communities have become a fading dream of the sixties and seventies, and have not proved to be the answer to the exhausting demands of small children and the survival of marriages. Instead divorce has become the most popular form of family survival and stepparents have taken on a lot of the burden of child rearing. But even if the foundations of a 'cooperative producing unit' is not possible in our present society, Chodorow does throw up a challenging discussion as to why we have become such a divorce-prone society. If we could imagine a more cooperative society in which shared parenting became the norm, perhaps we could imagine a benign circle surrounding our children, in which the input from many significant figures plays a part in the structuring of the psyche, rather than the more rigid roles imposed upon men and women in our capitalist society.

As is clear I have found many difficulties. I started out wondering why stepparents and stepmothers, in particular, had had such a bad image. I had imagined that exploring the history of the fairy story I should see that the stepmother had had imposed upon her centuries of false and imaginary misdemeanours. Unfortunately the high divorce rates in our present Western democracies and the proliferation of stepparents have reinvoked the persistent fairy tale image of the stepmother. I have found that our psychological theories and our understanding have gone to sleep over this increasingly common form of family structure. In 1975 Maddox wrote, 'Despite the growing number of remarriages with children, the field of stepfamily studies, just three decades or so old, is so new that it might be considered an emerging practice area.'[18] Thirty-five years later Wednesday Martin (2015) wrote that she had to struggle against being seen as a Stepmonster when she became a stepmother.[19] The ignorance has continued.

However Martin's message is optimistic about the consequences of divorce. She believes that this new kinship system can never be the same as a marriage that endures and in which the children are brought up. The mistake we have made, whether therapists or not, is to imagine that a good stepfamily can become like the original family. It cannot, and we are doing a disservice to everyone if we look at the stepfamily through the lens of an intact family.

When I wondered whether to call my book 'Beyond human strength' I thought that those words, written in the nineteenth century, were telling a truth. Now what Martin helps me to see is that in many ways Gladstone's words (quoted in Chapter 7) have been confirmed. To be a stepmother or stepfather requires a capacity of empathy and understanding beyond our imagination and beyond the imaginative expectation that most of us bring. Just to give one example, to be a stepparent is to be hated initially by your stepchildren, and that is fundamental and in some ways is a shocking beginning to a new marriage and a new family. A stepparent will only in time gain love and affection from the stepchildren. Furthermore there will be a constant irritant that will rub against the grain of the new partnership; the stepparent will be dealing with the guilt and pain of their partner and the broken psychic foundations of their original family.

My final view is that our psychological theories have ignored the important role that stepparents now play in our new kinship structures because of an over concentration on the minutiae of the inner world and the ignoring of outside reality. It has been fundamental to the development of our psychoanalytic thinking to separate out the inner world of fantasy and the unconscious mind from the values of our cultural life, but one result has been that there has not been enough dialogue or interchange between these two worlds. This type of splitting, between the outer world of cultural values and the inner world of imagination, has led to ignoring stepparents and their contributions to the structure of the psyche of their stepchildren, as though they were no more than parents in disguise, or should we say in 'wolves' clothing'?

It seems clear that if we just concentrate in our psychological theories on the early influence of the mother and father on the child's mental health we do not need to think about the influence of later stepparents. But I have begun to have an uncomfortable feeling that there may be another reason for the neglect of stepparents in our psychological understanding. We all seem to hold a negative image of them, especially the stepmother, and this may have hindered our thinking about them in our therapeutic work and in the transference. It seems possible that therapists may have wanted to avoid the feeling that at times they may be believed to be no better than a wicked stepmother. We do not like to imagine we 'smell' wrong, that the monetary demands we make reveal our predatory desires, or that we are seen as essentially unreliable because we are the 'wrong' person.

There is another uncomfortable feature that therapy can share with stepparenting. Therapists can never take the place of a parent, even if it is hoped we can become a benign influence slightly rearranging the furniture in the inner world of our clients and making them more familiar with their unconscious mind. Perhaps we have failed to face the fact that we are always at a stepparenting distance from them. A debate that has threaded its way throughout the history of psychoanalysis is about the therapist's place in the inner world of the client's psyche. Who are we, or who do we become? Perhaps one reason our theories have turned a blind eye to stepparents is because we shudder at the thought that we may be seen, at times, as a wicked stepmother or an incestuous stepfather. At such moments, if we have failed to recognize a stepchild/stepparent transference the therapy may come to an unexpected end. This leads to the idea that we need to recognize that stepfamilies play an increasingly important part in our society, and without the recognition of this fact, and its psychological consequences, the cultural heritage of the fairy story will continue to cloud our thinking and we may continue to be unconsciously driven by the fantasy that stepparents still want to harm their stepchildren 'in the secret inscriptions of the mind.'[20]

Notes

1. Gerhardt, S. (2017) *The Selfish Society: The Current State of Things* (p. 69). Benjamin Constant, writing in 1819, was also concerned that the culturally dominating libertarian view was 'market-based, individualist and consumerist.' Quoted in Bonneuil and Fressoz (2017) p. 41.
2. Sandel, M. (2012) *What Money Can't Buy.* Are we 'moving towards a society in which everything is up for sale?' (p. 8)
3. In Kent Haruf's (2015) posthumous novel *Our Souls at Night* he captured a dialogue that if it could be spoken might have helped: 'everything was at a cliff edge . . . I can't do this I said . . . This is going to hurt too many people. It has already. And here I am trying to be father to your daughter while my own is growing up without me. I have to go back because of her, if for no other reason' (p. 39). I am grateful to Dorothy Judd for suggesting I should read this novel.
4. Recent Relate Report. Out of 100,458 divorces in 2016, 20,000 could save their marriages with the right support. Available at www.relate.org.uk.
5. Quoted in Leach (2014) UK Office of National Statistics. 'The highest divorce percentages (well over 50%) are between the fourth and eighth year of marriage. The peak begins to drop around the tenth year' (p. xv).
6. Cusk (2012) p. 2.
7. Cusk (2012) p. 16.
8. Such a view finds support in T. Jackson (2010) who wrote that we are 'persuaded to spend money we don't have on things we don't need to make impressions that won't last on people we don't care about.' TED talk.
9. Gerhardt (2017) p. 69.
10. Leach (2014) p. 173.
11. Jacobs (2017) p. 31.
12. LeBey (2005) p. 67.
13. LeBey (2005) p. 80.
14. 'A brush with my daughter,' Philippe Morgese, *Guardian Family* (25 February 2017) p. 2.
15. Maxwell (2012). Available at: http://www.parentingacrossscotland.org/publications/essays-about-parenting/supporting-families-through-transition/parenting-after-separation-the-case-for-sharing/.
16. Nielsen (2011).
17. Chodorow (1978) pp. 3–4.
18. Maddox (1975) p. 28.
19. Martin (2015) p. 241.
20. De Quincey (2003 [1821]) p. 133.

References

Bonneuil, C. and Fressoz, J.-B. (2017) *The Shock of the Anthropocene.* London/New York: Verso.

Chodorow, N. (1978) *The Reproduction of Mothering.* California/London: University of California Press.

Cusk, R. (2012) *Aftermath: On Marriage and Separation.* London: Faber & Faber.

De Quincey, T. (2003 [1821]) *Confessions of an English Opium Eater and Other Writings.* Ed. B. Milligan. London: Penguin Books.

Gerhardt, S. (2017) The Selfish Society: The State of Things. In *The Political Self: Understanding the Social Context for Mental Illness.* Ed. R. Tweedy. London: Karnac Books Ltd.

Haruf, K. (2015) *Our Souls at Night.* New York/London: Picador.
Jackson, T (2010). An economic reality check. TED talk. Available at: https://www.ted.com/talks.tim_jackson_s_economc_reality_check/transcript? language=en.
Jacobs, A. (2017) Rethinking Matricide. In *The Mother in Psychoanalysis and Beyond.* Ed. R. Mayo and C. Moutsou. London/New York: Routledge.
Leach, P. (2014) *Family Breakdown: Helping Children to Hang on to Both Their Parents.* London: Unbound.
LeBey, B. (2005) *Re-Married with Children.* New York/Canada/Australia/London: Bantam Books.
Maddox, B. (1975) *The Half-Parent: Living with Other People's Children.* London: Andre Deutsch Ltd.
Maxwell, I. (2012) Parenting after separation: the case for sharing. Available at: http://www.parentingacrossscotland.org/publications/essays-about-parenting/supporting-families-through-transition/parenting-after-separation-the-case-for-sharing/.
Martin, W. (2015) *Stepmonster: A New Look at Why Real Stepmothers Think, Feel and Act the Way We Do.* Boston: Houghton Mifflin Harcourt.
Mayo, R. and Moutsou, C. (2017) Eds. *The Mother in Psychoanalysis and Beyond: Matricide and Maternal Subjectivity.* London/New York: Routledge.
Nielsen, L. (2011) Shared parenting after divorce: A review of shared residential parenting research. *Journal of Divorce & Remarriage.* 52. 8. 586–609.
Sandel, M.S. (2012) *What Money Can't Buy: The Moral Limits of Markets.* London: Penguin Books.

Index

adultery 33, 37–39
Aesop's fables 6
Allerleirauh 22
Allison, Elizabeth 92
annihilation anxiety 79
anxiety: annihilation anxiety 79; castration anxiety 40; Oedipus myth 103; in stepchildren 48, 49, 51, 79, 103; towards women 33–37, 41, 45
Arthur, King 37
Asquith, Margot 84
Athena 34, 112
attachment: absence in stepfamilies 11, 46–47; impact of trauma 86–87; implications for therapy 110; insecure attachment 77–78; new kinship systems 89–90; psychological needs 114; stepparent jealousy 48; wet nurses and nannies 71, 95–96

Basile, Giambattista 9
Beauty and the Beast 6
Bettelheim, Bruno 1, 19, 24–25, 26, 75–77, 92
'black hole' 78–79
bourgeoisie 10, 20–21
Bowlby, John 77
Bray, James 85
breastfeeding 91–92
Byron, Lord 62–63

castration anxiety 40
Chaucer, Geoffrey 36
childrearing practices 11, 13
children/stepchildren: anxiety 48, 49, 51, 79, 103; impacts of divorce 3, 46–47, 53–54, 72, 78, 79, 85–88, 91, 96, 99, 102–103; psychic moorings 45–54; sexual development 28, 49–50, 53–54, 72

China 8
Chodorow, Nancy 114–115
Christianity 1–2, 35, 36
Church, Elizabeth 100
Cinderella 7–15; Bettelheim's analysis 75–76; Freudian analysis 8, 74–75; historical adaptation 1–2, 8–10; Mary Shelley parallels 61, 67, 68; origins 1–2, 7–8, 75; stepmother archetype 6, 7, 8, 39; *see also* Donkey-Skin; Zezolla
Clairmont, Jane (later Claire) 57, 61, 62–64
Clairmont, Mary-Jane 3, 57–68
Clarke, Kenneth 12
Codrington, Helen 39
conflict: psychological 63, 72, 74, 97; relational 64, 74, 75, 90–91, 95, 98, 101, 103, 104, 109
Cupid and Psyche 12
Cusk, Rachel 111–112

Daly, Martin 96–97, 98
David, Frederich 77
death: and attachment 87; of a child 65; in Cinderella narrative 74–75; of a mother 2, 15, 46, 47, 57, 65, 67, 68, 75, 76; of a spouse 58; stepmother associated with 37
desire: incestuous 22–23, 25, 26–27, 52, 64, 65, 66–68, 76; male 27, 112; Oedipal 25, 47, 76, 80; sexual 28, 39, 49, 50, 52–54; women 14, 35, 36–37, 39–40
Disney 12, 39
divorce: impacts on children 3, 46–47, 53–54, 72, 78, 79, 85–88, 91, 96, 99, 102–103; impacts on divorcing parties 98, 110–112, 113; inheritance rights

11, 97; intergenerational repetition 90, 102–103; as liberation 72, 100, 102; medieval law 38; prevalence 4, 54, 71, 90, 109, 110, 111, 115; after second marriage 90; shared parenting 114–115; *see also* new kinship systems; second marriages

Divorce Law (1857) 38, 39

Donkey-Skin: Bettelheim's analysis 76; incestuous desire 22, 27, 52, 76; Mary Shelley parallels 57, 65, 68; as 'old wives' tale' 23, 24

Enlightenment, the 33

Euripides 83

fairy godmother 23

fairy stories: Bettelheim's analysis 75–77, 92; fathers/stepfathers in 2, 6, 19–28, 98, 116; origins 2, 6; power 6, 15; psychoanalytic perspectives 3, 25–26; social and cultural adaptation 1–2, 8–9, 14, 15, 19–22, 26, 27–28; stepmothers in 1, 5–15, 45, 57, 115, 116

families: changing structures 77, 84–85, 87, 88–89, 91, 103; Freudian perspectives 72–73; ideals 2, 71, 95; power struggles 75

fantasy: concerning parents 53, 67, 91; concerning stepmothers 10–11, 15, 40, 73; and fairy stories 3; incestuous desire 52, 67; in marriage 111; and reality 10, 25, 72, 92, 103, 116; sexual development 53, 72

fathers/stepfathers: Bettelheim's analysis 75–76; children's anxieties 47, 48, 52–53, 104, 113; in fairy stories 2, 6, 19–28, 31, 98, 116; incestuous desires 22–23, 26–27, 52, 65, 66–68, 76; post-bereavement 10; post-divorce 113–114; sexual abuse by 25, 26; *see also* Godwin, William

favouritism 85–86

Fonagy, Peter 92

Fraiberg, Selma 102

Freud, Sigmund: castration anxiety 40; child psyche 28; Cinderella 8, 9, 74–75; fathers/stepfathers 25–26, 27; female psyche 34; limitations of theory 25, 72, 77

Gaskell, Elizabeth 2, 45–54, 90

Gerhardt, Sue 4, 98, 109, 112

Germany 20–21

Gibson, Molly 2, 46–54, 84

Gladstone, William 84, 90, 115

goddesses 2, 31–34, 45, 74–75

Godwin, Mary *see* Shelley, Mary

Godwin, William 3, 57–58, 60–61, 66–68

Gorell Barnes, Gill 3, 87, 89–90

Greek mythology 31–34

Grimm Brothers 8, 15, 20–21, 23, 34

group therapy 109–110

Hansel and Gretel 2, 8

Hera 31–34, 36, 41, 45

Herakles 33–34, 45

Hetherington, E. Mavis 3

Homer 34

human rights 72, 87

Imlay, Fanny 57, 58, 59, 61–62

incestuous desire 22–23, 26–27, 52, 64, 65, 66–68, 76

individual therapy 109–110

industrialization 21

inheritance rights 11, 97

Jacobs, Amber 4, 34, 112

jealousy: parents for children 49, 53, 66, 67; between siblings/stepsiblings 10, 64; stepmother archetype 5, 8, 12, 31, 32, 34, 36, 48, 52; between women 8, 10, 13

Kelly, John 3, 85

Lamb, Charles 59

Leach, Penelope 4, 112, 114

LeBey, Barbara 113

Lewis, Julia 74, 79, 84

Little Red Riding Hood 24–25, 76

loss, of a mother 7, 10–11, 15, 75, 89

Mackenzie, Donald 32

Maddox, Brenda 84, 88, 89, 90, 115

The Maiden without Hands 23

Mandeville (Godwin) 68

Manfred (Byron) 68

marriage 12, 21, 72, 77, 100, 111; *see also* divorce; second marriages

Martin, Wednesday 100, 115

Masson, J. M. 25

materialism 4, 109, 110

Mathilda (Shelley) 65–68

McGilchrist, Iain 77

McGregor, Neil 20–21

Mead, Margaret 84

men *see* fathers/stepfathers
Metis 112–113
Mill, J. S. 72, 88, 100, 102
mothers: idealization of 2, 8, 10, 14, 21, 22; loss of 2, 7, 10–11, 13–15, 21, 40, 47, 57, 65, 67–68, 75, 89; psychoanalytic perspectives 72, 113; therapeutic needs 112
mothers-in-law 12, 13, 26, 104

nannies 7, 11, 71, 72, 95
New Fathers 4 Justice 114
new kinship systems 84, 88–90, 96, 102, 105, 115–116
Nielsen, Linda 114
Norton, Caroline 38–39
nuclear family 72

Oedipal desire 25, 47, 76, 80
Oedipus 103
'old wives' tales' 13, 21, 23, 24, 26
oral tales 1–3, 6, 8, 19–20, 26–28, 76–77; *see also* fairy stories

Panksepp, Jaak 77
patriarchy 14, 21, 23, 33, 36, 112
Perrault, Charles 10, 15, 23
Perry, Grayson 79–80, 83
psychic moorings 45–54, 73, 84

Queen Mab (Shelley) 68
Queen of Sheba 35–36

Reformation, the 21
Robinson, Margaret 71, 88, 89, 100
Rutter, Michael 77

Sandel, Michael 109
Schore, Allan 77
second marriages 47–48, 52–53, 90–91, 100, 103–104, 110–111
'selfish society' 4, 109–110, 112
sexual abuse 25–28
sexuality: child development 28, 49–50, 53–54, 72; Cinderella narrative 8, 10, 12; fathers 23, 27–28; Freudian perspectives 25, 40; parent–child dynamics 53; stepmother archetype 35, 37, 39, 41; stepsiblings 64; *see also* desire
'shadows' 52–53
Shelley, Mary 3, 57–68
Shelley, Percy Bysshe 3, 57, 59, 62–63, 66
Snow White 8

Solomon, King 35–36
Sophocles 103
Spark, Muriel 64
stepchildren *see* children/stepchildren
stepfathers *see* fathers/stepfathers
stepmothers: attachment theory 77–78; as 'aunts' 100; Bettelheim's analysis 75–76; in fairy stories 1, 5–15, 45, 57, 115, 116; fear projection 32, 41; in pagan mythology 31–33; psychic moorings 73, 84; relationship with stepchildren 97–98, 101, 104; as scapegoat for mother 8, 10, 13–14, 21, 73, 75, 92, 102; as 'second mother' 2, 7, 45, 48, 52, 90, 91; sexuality 35, 37, 39, 41; 'wicked' archetype 1–2, 5–15, 21, 23, 34, 59, 68, 75, 116
stepsiblings 9–10, 50, 61–64
Stone, Lawrence 19
Strout, Elizabeth 72

Tatar, Maria 22
Taylor, Edgar 20
therapy: case examples 73–74, 78–80, 86, 89, 98–101, 103–104; historical limitations and future directions 71, 77, 88–89, 91–92, 116; individual and group 109–110; stepparent transference 73–74, 79–80, 95, 98–99
transference 3, 73–74, 79–80, 83, 88–89, 95, 98–99, 116
trauma 78–79, 87, 96, 99

Virgin Mary 36

Wallerstein, Judith 3, 46–47, 74, 79, 84, 85–88
Warner, Marina 13, 15, 19, 26
wet nurses 7, 11, 13, 71, 72, 95
widows 11–12
Wilson, Margo 96–97, 98
Wives and Daughters (Gaskell) 45–54
Wollstonecraft, Mary 57, 60
women: desires 14, 35–37, 39–40; fear of 2, 13–14, 23, 32–37, 41, 45; historical and cultural perceptions 31–41, 68; and patriarchy 20, 112; rights 72, 87, 100, 112; as storytellers 13–14, 23, 24, 26; *see also* mothers; stepmothers

Zeus 31–32, 33, 34–35, 41, 45, 112–113
Zezolla 9, 14, 22
Zipes, Jack 6, 19

Taylor & Francis eBooks

Helping you to choose the right eBooks for your Library

Add Routledge titles to your library's digital collection today. Taylor and Francis ebooks contains over 50,000 titles in the Humanities, Social Sciences, Behavioural Sciences, Built Environment and Law.

Choose from a range of subject packages or create your own!

Benefits for you
- Free MARC records
- COUNTER-compliant usage statistics
- Flexible purchase and pricing options
- All titles DRM-free.

Benefits for your user
- Off-site, anytime access via Athens or referring URL
- Print or copy pages or chapters
- Full content search
- Bookmark, highlight and annotate text
- Access to thousands of pages of quality research at the click of a button.

REQUEST YOUR FREE INSTITUTIONAL TRIAL TODAY

Free Trials Available
We offer free trials to qualifying academic, corporate and government customers.

eCollections – Choose from over 30 subject eCollections, including:

Archaeology	Language Learning
Architecture	Law
Asian Studies	Literature
Business & Management	Media & Communication
Classical Studies	Middle East Studies
Construction	Music
Creative & Media Arts	Philosophy
Criminology & Criminal Justice	Planning
Economics	Politics
Education	Psychology & Mental Health
Energy	Religion
Engineering	Security
English Language & Linguistics	Social Work
Environment & Sustainability	Sociology
Geography	Sport
Health Studies	Theatre & Performance
History	Tourism, Hospitality & Events

For more information, pricing enquiries or to order a free trial, please contact your local sales team: **www.tandfebooks.com/page/sales**

The home of Routledge books

www.tandfebooks.com

For Product Safety Concerns and Information please contact our EU
representative GPSR@taylorandfrancis.com
Taylor & Francis Verlag GmbH, Kaufingerstraße 24, 80331 München, Germany

www.ingramcontent.com/pod-product-compliance
Lightning Source LLC
Chambersburg PA
CBHW051404290426
44108CB00015B/2153